I0009586

Amazon Simple Storage Service Console User Guide

A catalogue record for this book is available from the Hong Kong Public Libraries.

Published in Hong Kong by Samurai Media Limited.

Email: info@samuraimedia.org

ISBN 9789888408504

Copyright 2018 Amazon Web Services, Inc. and/or its affiliates.
Minor modifications for publication Copyright 2018 Samurai Media Limited.

This book is licensed under the Creative Commons Attribution-ShareAlike 4.0 International Public License.

Background Cover Image by https://www.flickr.com/people/webtreatsetc/

Contents

Welcome to the Amazon S3 Console User Guide

Welcome to the *Amazon Simple Storage Service Console User Guide* for the Amazon Simple Storage Service (Amazon S3) console.

Amazon S3 provides virtually limitless storage on the internet. This guide explains how you can manage buckets, objects, and folders in Amazon S3 by using the AWS Management Console, a browser-based graphical user interface for interacting with AWS services.

For detailed conceptual information about how Amazon S3 works, see What Is Amazon S3? in the *Amazon Simple Storage Service Developer Guide*. The developer guide also has detailed information about Amazon S3 features and code examples to support those features.

Topics

- Creating and Configuring an S3 Bucket
- Uploading, Downloading, and Managing Objects
- Storage Management
- Setting Bucket and Object Access Permissions

Creating and Configuring an S3 Bucket

Amazon S3 is cloud storage for the Internet. To upload your data (photos, videos, documents etc.), you first create a bucket in one of the AWS Regions. You can then upload your data objects to the bucket.

Every object you store in Amazon S3 resides in a bucket. You can use buckets to group related objects in the same way that you use a directory to group files in a file system.

Amazon S3 creates buckets in the AWS Region that you specify. You can choose any AWS Region that is geographically close to you to optimize latency, minimize costs, or address regulatory requirements. For example, if you reside in Europe, you might find it advantageous to create buckets in the EU (Ireland) or EU (Frankfurt) regions. For a list of Amazon S3 AWS Regions, see Regions and Endpoints in the *Amazon Web Services General Reference*.

You are not charged for creating a bucket. You are only charged for storing objects in the bucket and for transferring objects out of the bucket. For more information about pricing, see Amazon Simple Storage Service (S3) FAQs.

Amazon S3 bucket names are globally unique, regardless of the AWS Region in which you create the bucket. You specify the name at the time you create the bucket. For bucket naming guidelines, see Bucket Restrictions and Limitations in the *Amazon Simple Storage Service Developer Guide*.

The following topics explain how to use the Amazon S3 console to create, delete, and manage buckets.

How Do I Create an S3 Bucket?

Before you can upload data to Amazon S3, you must create a bucket in one of the AWS Regions to store your data in. After you create a bucket, you can upload an unlimited number of data objects to the bucket.

Buckets have configuration properties, including their geographical region, who has access to the objects in the bucket, and other metadata.

To create an S3 bucket

1. Sign in to the AWS Management Console and open the Amazon S3 console at https://console.aws.amazon.com/s3/.

2. Choose **Create bucket**.

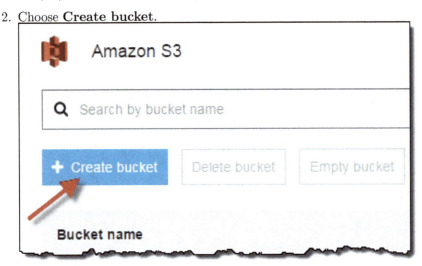

3. On the **Name and region** page, type a name for your bucket and choose the AWS Region where you want the bucket to reside. Complete the fields on this page as follows:

   1. For **Bucket name**, type a unique DNS-compliant name for your new bucket. Follow these naming guidelines:

      - The name must be unique across all existing bucket names in Amazon S3.

      - The name must not contain uppercase characters.

      - The name must start with a lowercase letter or number.

      - The name must be between 3 and 63 characters long.

      - After you create the bucket you cannot change the name, so choose wisely.

      - Choose a bucket name that reflects the objects in the bucket because the bucket name is visible in the URL that points to the objects that you're going to put in your bucket.

      For information about naming buckets, see Rules for Bucket Naming in the *Amazon Simple Storage Service Developer Guide*.

   2. For **Region**, choose the AWS Region where you want the bucket to reside. Choose a Region close to you to minimize latency and costs, or to address regulatory requirements. Objects stored in a Region never leave that Region unless you explicitly transfer them to another Region. For a list of Amazon S3 AWS Regions, see Regions and Endpoints in the *Amazon Web Services General Reference*.

   3. (Optional) If you have already set up a bucket that has the same settings that you want to use for the new bucket that you want to create, you can set it up quickly by choosing **Copy settings from an existing bucket**, and then choosing the bucket whose settings you want to copy.

The settings for the following bucket properties are copied: versioning, tags, and logging.

4. Do one of the following:

   - If you copied settings from another bucket, choose **Create**. You're done, so skip the following steps.

   - If not, choose **Next**.

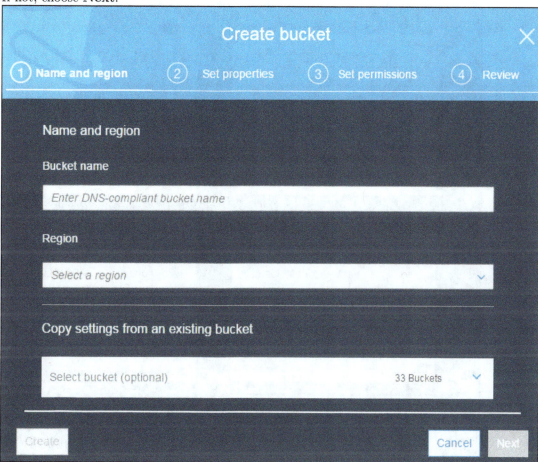

4. On the **Set properties** page, you can configure the following properties for the bucket. Or, you can configure these properties later, after you create the bucket.

   1. **Versioning** – Versioning enables you to keep multiple versions of an object in one bucket. Versioning is disabled for a new bucket by default. For information on enabling versioning, see How Do I Enable or Suspend Versioning for an S3 Bucket?.

   2. **Server access logging** – Server access logging provides detailed records for the requests that are made to your bucket. By default, Amazon S3 does not collect server access logs. For information about enabling server access logging, see How Do I Enable Server Access Logging for an S3 Bucket?.

   3. **Tags** – With AWS cost allocation, you can use tags to annotate billing for your use of a bucket. A tag is a key-value pair that represents a label that you assign to a bucket. To add tags, choose **Tags**, and then choose **Add tag**. For more information, see Using Cost Allocation Tags for S3 Buckets in the *Amazon Simple Storage Service Developer Guide*.

   4. **Object-level logging** – Object-level logging records object-level API activity by using CloudTrail data events. For information about enabling object-level logging, see How Do I Enable Object-Level Logging for an S3 Bucket with AWS CloudTrail Data Events?.

   5. **Default encryption** – Amazon S3 default encryption provides a way to set the default encryption

behavior for an S3 bucket. You can set default encryption on a bucket so that all objects are encrypted when they are stored in the bucket. For information about enabling default encryption, see How Do I Enable Default Encryption for an S3 Bucket?.

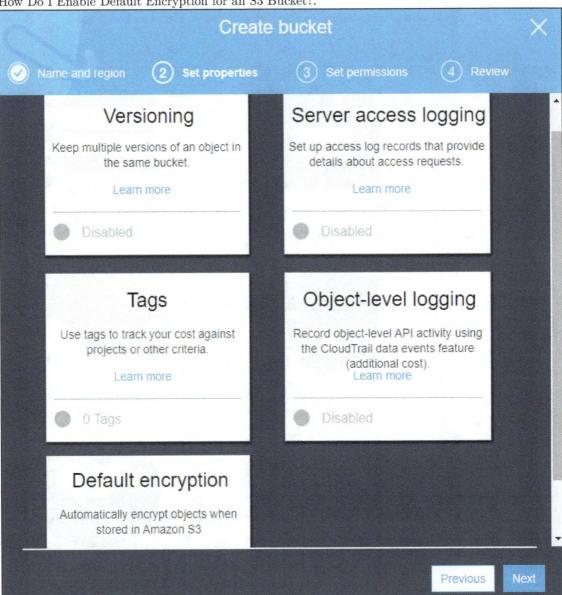

5. Choose **Next**.

6. On the **Set permissions** page, you manage the permissions that are set on the bucket that you are creating. You can grant read access to your bucket to the general public (everyone in the world). Granting public read access is applicable to a small subset of use cases such as when buckets are used for websites. We recommend that you do not change the default setting of **Do not grant public read access to this bucket**. You can change permissions after you create the bucket. For more information about setting bucket permissions, see How Do I Set ACL Bucket Permissions? **Warning**
We highly recommend that you *do not* grant public read access to the bucket that you are creating. Granting public read access permissions means that anyone in the world can access the objects in the bucket.

When you're done configuring permissions on the bucket, choose **Next**.

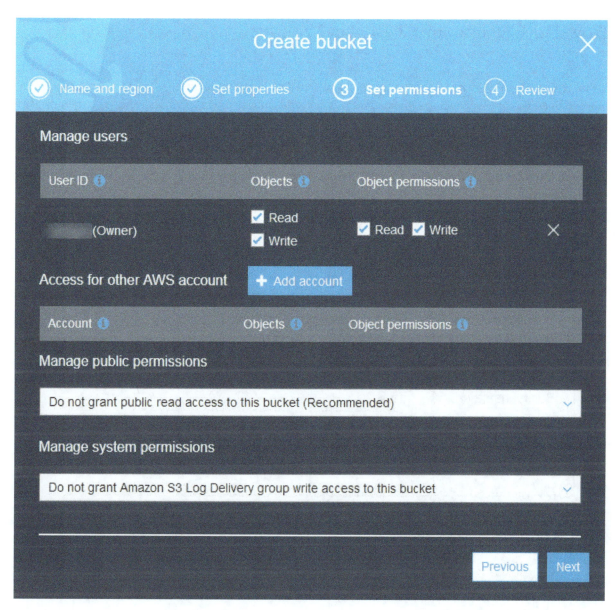

7. On the **Review** page, verify the settings. If you want to change something, choose **Edit**. If your current settings are correct, choose **Create bucket**.

More Info

- How Do I Delete an S3 Bucket?
- How Do I Set ACL Bucket Permissions?

How Do I Delete an S3 Bucket?

You can delete a bucket and all of the objects contained in the bucket. You can also delete an empty bucket. When you delete a bucket with versioning enabled, all versions of all the objects in the bucket are deleted. For more information, see Managing Objects in a Versioning-Enabled Bucket and Deleting/Emptying a Bucket in the *Amazon Simple Storage Service Developer Guide*.

Important

If you want to continue to use the same bucket name, don't delete the bucket. We recommend that you empty the bucket and keep it. After a bucket is deleted, the name becomes available to reuse, but the name might not be available for you to reuse for various reasons. For example, it might take some time before the name can be reused and some other account could create a bucket with that name before you do.

To delete an S3 bucket

1. Sign in to the AWS Management Console and open the Amazon S3 console at https://console.aws.amazon.com/s3/.

2. In the **Bucket name** list, choose the bucket icon next to the name of the bucket that you want to delete and then choose **Delete bucket**.

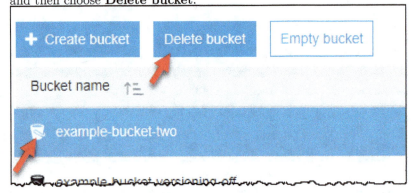

3. In the **Delete bucket** dialog box, type the name of the bucket that you want to delete for confirmation and then choose **Confirm**.

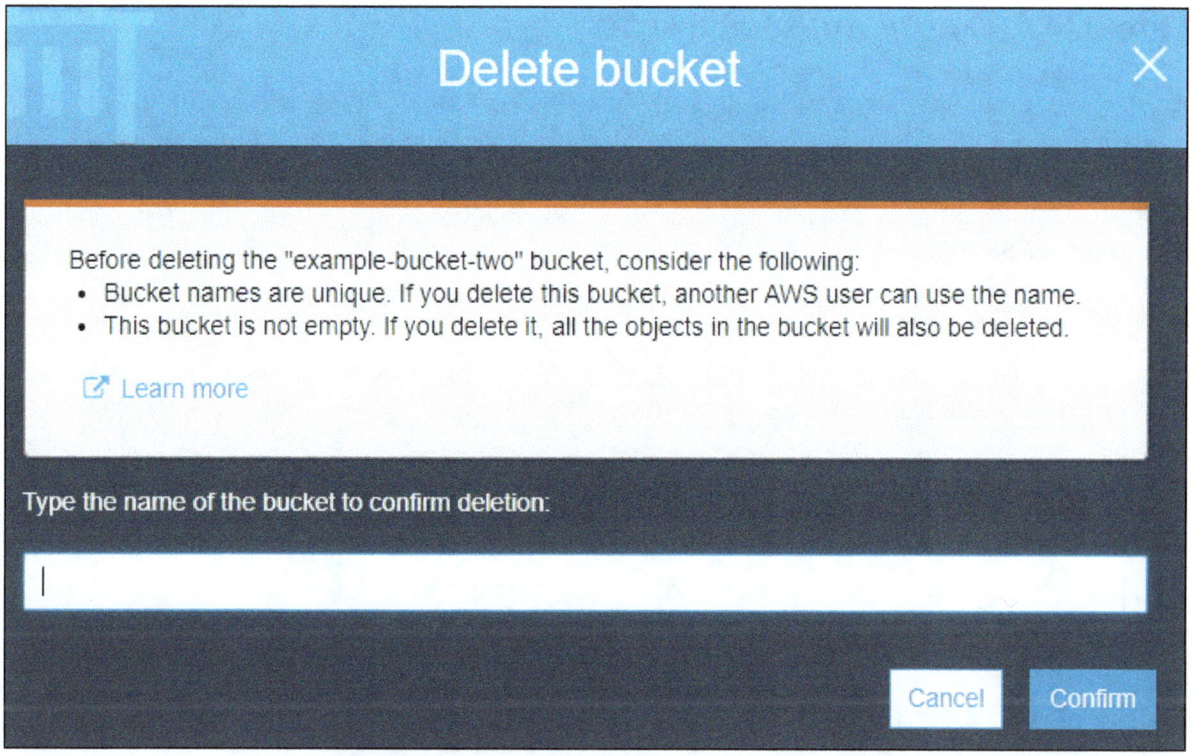

Delete bucket

Before deleting the "example-bucket-two" bucket, consider the following:
- Bucket names are unique. If you delete this bucket, another AWS user can use the name.
- This bucket is not empty. If you delete it, all the objects in the bucket will also be deleted.

☐ Learn more

Type the name of the bucket to confirm deletion:

|

Cancel   Confirm

How Do I Empty an S3 Bucket?

You can empty a bucket, which deletes all of the objects in the bucket without deleting the bucket. When you empty a bucket with versioning enabled, all versions of all the objects in the bucket are deleted. For more information, see Managing Objects in a Versioning-Enabled Bucket and Deleting/Emptying a Bucket in the *Amazon Simple Storage Service Developer Guide*.

To empty an S3 bucket

1. Sign in to the AWS Management Console and open the Amazon S3 console at https://console.aws.amazon.com/s3/.

2. In the **Bucket name** list, choose the bucket icon next to the name of the bucket that you want to delete and then choose **Empty bucket**.

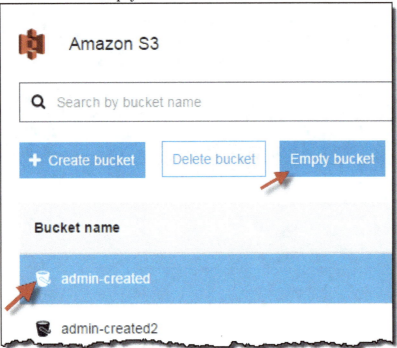

3. In the **Empty bucket** dialog box, type the name of the bucket you want to empty for confirmation and then choose **Confirm**.

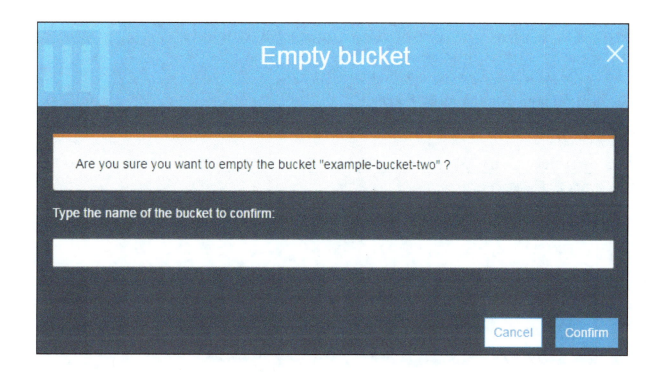

Empty bucket ✕

Are you sure you want to empty the bucket "example-bucket-two" ?

Type the name of the bucket to confirm:

Cancel   Confirm

How Do I View the Properties for an S3 Bucket?

This topic explains how to view the properties for an S3 bucket.

To view the properties for an S3 bucket

1. Sign in to the AWS Management Console and open the Amazon S3 console at https://console.aws.amazon.com/s3/.

2. In the **Bucket name** list, choose the name of the bucket that you want to view the properties for.

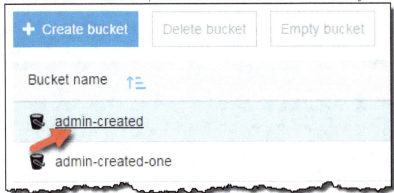

3. Choose **Properties**.

4. On the **Properties** page, you can configure the following properties for the bucket.

   1. **Versioning** – Versioning enables you to keep multiple versions of an object in one bucket. By default, versioning is disabled for a new bucket. For information about enabling versioning, see How Do I Enable or Suspend Versioning for an S3 Bucket?.

   2. **Server access logging** – Server access logging provides detailed records for the requests that are made to your bucket. By default, Amazon S3 does not collect server access logs. For information about enabling server access logging, see How Do I Enable Server Access Logging for an S3 Bucket?.

   3. **Static website hosting** – You can host a static website on Amazon S3. To enable static website hosting, choose **Static website hosting** and then specify the settings you want to use. For more information, see How Do I Configure an S3 Bucket for Static Website Hosting?.

   4. **Object-level logging** – Object-level logging records object-level API activity by using CloudTrail data events. For information about enabling object-level logging, see How Do I Enable Object-Level Logging for an S3 Bucket with AWS CloudTrail Data Events?.

   5. **Tags** – With AWS cost allocation, you can use bucket tags to annotate billing for your use of a bucket. A tag is a key-value pair that represents a label that you assign to a bucket. To add tags, choose **Tags**, and then choose **Add tag**. For more information, see Using Cost Allocation Tags for S3 Buckets in the *Amazon Simple Storage Service Developer Guide*.

   6. **Transfer acceleration** – Amazon S3 Transfer Acceleration enables fast, easy, and secure transfers of files over long distances between your client and an S3 bucket. For information about enabling transfer acceleration, see How Do I Enable Transfer Acceleration for an S3 Bucket?.

   7. **Events** – You can enable certain Amazon S3 bucket events to send a notification message to a destination whenever the events occur. To enable events, choose **Events** and then specify the settings

you want to use. For more information, see How Do I Enable and Configure Event Notifications for an S3 Bucket?.

8. **Requester Pays** – You can enable Requester Pays so that the requester (instead of the bucket owner) pays for requests and data transfers. For more information, see Requester Pays Buckets in the *Amazon Simple Storage Service Developer Guide.*

How Do I Enable or Suspend Versioning for an S3 Bucket?

Versioning enables you to keep multiple versions of an object in one bucket. This section describes how to enable object versioning on a bucket. For more information about versioning support in Amazon S3, see Object Versioning and Using Versioning in the *Amazon Simple Storage Service Developer Guide*.

To enable or disable versioning on an S3 bucket

1. Sign in to the AWS Management Console and open the Amazon S3 console at https://console.aws.amazon.com/s3/.

2. In the **Bucket name** list, choose the name of the bucket that you want to enable versioning for.

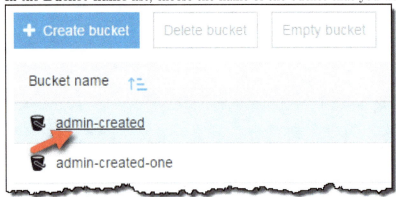

3. Choose **Properties**.

4. Choose **Versioning**.

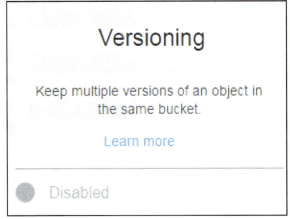

5. Choose **Enable versioning** or **Suspend versioning**, and then choose **Save**.

Versioning

✕

○ Enable versioning

⦿ Suspend versioning

This suspends the creation of object versions for all operations but preserves any existing object versions.

Cancel   Save

How Do I Enable Default Encryption for an S3 Bucket?

Amazon S3 default encryption provides a way to set the default encryption behavior for an S3 bucket. You can set default encryption on a bucket so that all objects are encrypted when they are stored in the bucket. The objects are encrypted using server-side encryption with either Amazon S3-managed keys (SSE-S3) or AWS KMS-managed keys (SSE-KMS).

When you use server-side encryption, Amazon S3 encrypts an object before saving it to disk in its data centers and decrypts it when you download the objects. For more information about protecting data using server-side encryption and encryption key management, see Protecting Data Using Server-Side Encryption in the *Amazon Simple Storage Service Developer Guide*.

Default encryption works with all existing and new S3 buckets. Without default encryption, to encrypt all objects stored in a bucket, you must include encryption information with every object storage request. You must also set up an S3 bucket policy to reject storage requests that don't include encryption information.

There are no new charges for using default encryption for S3 buckets. Requests to configure the default encryption feature incur standard Amazon S3 request charges. For information about pricing, see Amazon S3 Pricing. For SSE-KMS encryption key storage, AWS Key Management Service (AWS KMS) charges apply and are listed at AWS KMS Pricing.

To enable default encryption on an S3 bucket

1. Sign in to the AWS Management Console and open the Amazon S3 console at https://console.aws.amazon.com/s3/.

2. In the **Bucket name** list, choose the name of the bucket that you want.

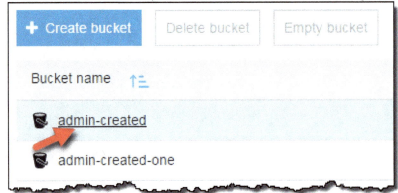

3. Choose **Properties**.

4. Choose **Default encryption**.

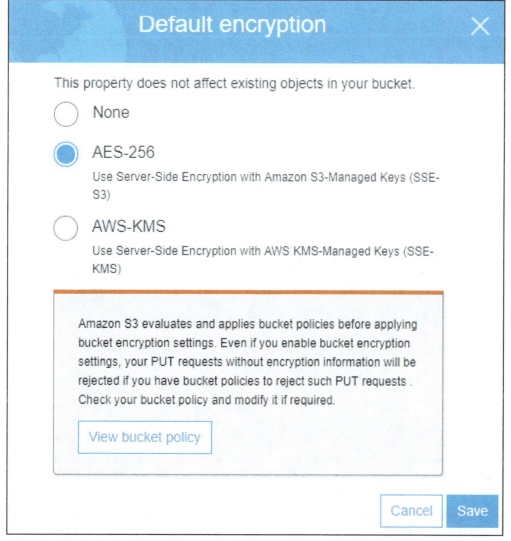

5. Choose **AES-256** or **AWS-KMS**.

   1. To use keys that are managed by Amazon S3 for default encryption, choose **AES-256**. For more information about using Amazon S3 server-side encryption to encrypt your data, see Protecting Data with Amazon S3-Managed Encryption Keys in the *Amazon Simple Storage Service Developer Guide*.

**Impor-
tant**

You might need to update your bucket policy when enabling default encryption. For more information, see Moving to Default Encryption from Using Bucket Policies for Encryption Enforcement in the *Amazon Simple Storage Service Developer Guide.*

2. To use keys that are managed by AWS KMS for default encryption, choose **AWS-KMS**, and then choose a master key from the list of the AWS KMS master keys that you have created. Type the Amazon Resource Name (ARN) of the AWS KMS key to use. You can find the ARN for your AWS KMS key in the IAM console, under **Encryption keys**. Or, you can choose a key name from the drop-down list.

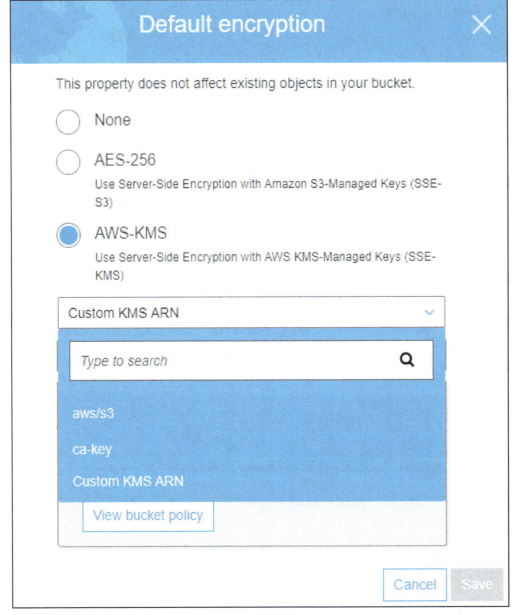

Impor-
tant
If you use the AWS KMS option for your default encryption configuration, you are subject to the RPS (requests per second) limits of AWS KMS. For more information about AWS KMS limits and how to request a limit increase, see AWS KMS limits.

For more information about creating an AWS KMS key, see Creating Keys in the *AWS Key Management Service Developer Guide.* For more information about using AWS KMS with Amazon S3, see Protecting Data with AWS KMS–Managed Keys in the *Amazon Simple Storage Service Developer Guide.*

6. Choose **Save**.

More Info

- Amazon S3 Default Encryption for S3 Buckets in the *Amazon Simple Storage Service Developer Guide*
- How Do I Add Encryption to an S3 Object?

How Do I Enable Server Access Logging for an S3 Bucket?

Server access logging provides detailed records for the requests made to a bucket. Server access logs are useful for many applications because they give bucket owners insight into the nature of requests made by clients not under their control. By default, Amazon Simple Storage Service (Amazon S3) doesn't collect server access logs. This topic describes how to enable logging for a bucket. For more information, see Server Access Logging in the *Amazon Simple Storage Service Developer Guide*.

When you enable logging, Amazon S3 delivers access logs to a target bucket that you choose. An access log record contains details about the requests made to a bucket. This can include the request type, the resources specified in the request, and the time and date the request was processed. For more information, see Server Access Log Format in the *Amazon Simple Storage Service Developer Guide*.

Important

There is no extra charge for enabling server access logging on an Amazon S3 bucket. However, any log files that the system delivers to you will accrue the usual charges for storage. (You can delete the log files at any time.) We do not assess data transfer charges for log file delivery, but we do charge the normal data transfer rate for accessing the log files.

To enable server access logging for an S3 bucket

1. Sign in to the AWS Management Console and open the Amazon S3 console at https://console.aws.amazon.com/s3/.

2. In the **Bucket name** list, choose the name of the bucket that you want to enable server access logging for.

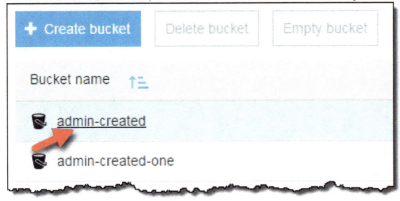

3. Choose **Properties**.

4. Choose **Server access logging**.

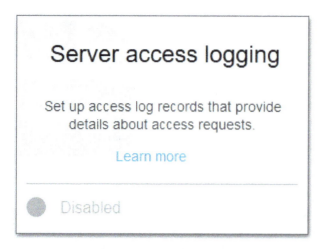

5. Choose **Enable Logging**. For **Target**, choose the name of the bucket that you want to receive the log record objects.

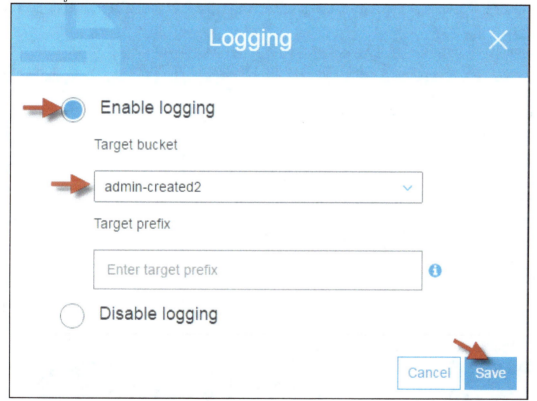

6. (Optional) For **Target prefix**, type a key name prefix for log objects, so that all of the log objects begin with the same string.

7. Choose **Save**.

More Info
How Do I View the Properties for an S3 Bucket?

How Do I Enable Object-Level Logging for an S3 Bucket with AWS CloudTrail Data Events?

This section describes how to enable an AWS CloudTrail trail to log data events for objects in an S3 bucket by using the Amazon S3 console. CloudTrail supports logging Amazon S3 object-level API operations such as `GetObject`, `DeleteObject`, and `PutObject`. These events are called data events. By default, CloudTrail trails don't log data events, but you can configure trails to log data events for S3 buckets that you specify, or to log data events for all the Amazon S3 buckets in your AWS account.

Important
Additional charges apply for data events. For more information, see AWS CloudTrail Pricing.

To configure a trail to log data events for an S3 bucket, you can use either the AWS CloudTrail console or the Amazon S3 console. If you are configuring a trail to log data events for all the Amazon S3 buckets in your AWS account, it's easier to use the CloudTrail console. For information about using the CloudTrail console to configure a trail to log S3 data events, see Data Events in the *AWS CloudTrail User Guide.*

The following procedure shows how to use the Amazon S3 console to enable a CloudTrail trail to log data events for an S3 bucket.

To enable CloudTrail data events logging for objects in an S3 bucket

1. Sign in to the AWS Management Console and open the Amazon S3 console at https://console.aws.amazon.com/s3/.

2. In the **Bucket name** list, choose the name of the bucket that you want.

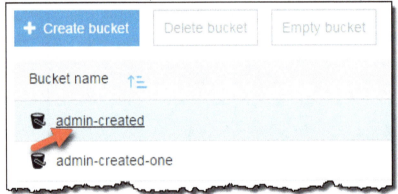

3. Choose **Properties**.

4. Choose **Object-level logging**.

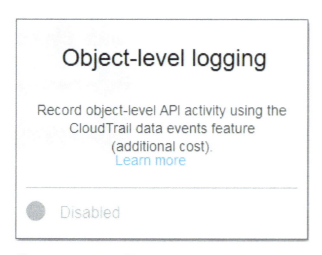

5. Choose an existing CloudTrail trail in the drop-down menu. The trail you select must be in the same AWS Region as your bucket, so the drop-down list contains only trails that are in the same Region as the bucket or trails that were created for all Regions.

   If you need to create a trail, choose the **CloudTrail console** link to go to the CloudTrail console. For information about how to create trails in the CloudTrail console, see Creating a Trail with the Console in the *AWS CloudTrail User Guide.*

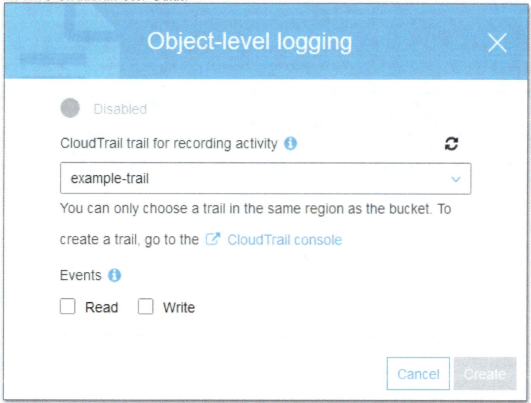

6. Under **Events**, select **Read** to specify that you want CloudTrail to log Amazon S3 read APIs such as GetObject. Select **Write** to log Amazon S3 write APIs such as PutObject. Select both **Read** and **Write** to log both read and write object APIs. For a list of supported data events that CloudTrail logs for Amazon S3 objects, see Amazon S3 Object-Level Actions Tracked by CloudTrail Logging in the *Amazon Simple Storage Service Developer Guide.*

7. Choose **Create** to enable object-level logging for the bucket.

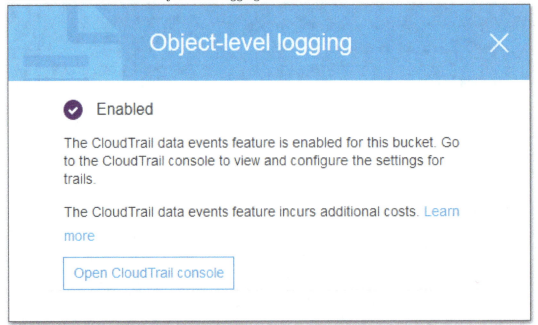

To disable object-level logging for the bucket, you must go to the CloudTrail console and remove the bucket name from the trail's **Data events**. **Note**
If you use the CloudTrail console or the Amazon S3 console to configure a trail to log data events for an S3 bucket, the Amazon S3 console shows that object-level logging is enabled for the bucket.

For information about enabling object-level logging when you create an S3 bucket, see How Do I Create an S3 Bucket?.

More Info

- How Do I View the Properties for an S3 Bucket?
- Logging Amazon S3 API Calls By Using AWS CloudTrail in the *Amazon Simple Storage Service Developer Guide*
- Working with CloudTrail Log Files in the *AWS CloudTrail User Guide*

How Do I Configure an S3 Bucket for Static Website Hosting?

You can host a static website on Amazon S3. On a static website, individual web pages include static content and they might also contain client-side scripts. By contrast, a dynamic website relies on server-side processing, including server-side scripts such as PHP, JSP, or ASP.NET. Amazon S3 does not support server-side scripting.

The following is a quick procedure to configure an Amazon S3 bucket for static website hosting in the S3 console. If you're looking for more in-depth information, as well as walkthroughs on using a custom domain name for your static website or speeding up your website, see Hosting a Static Website on Amazon S3 in the *Amazon Simple Storage Service Developer Guide*.

To configure an S3 bucket for static website hosting

1. Sign in to the AWS Management Console and open the Amazon S3 console at https://console.aws.amazon.com/s3/.

2. In the **Bucket name** list, choose the name of the bucket that you want to enable static website hosting for.

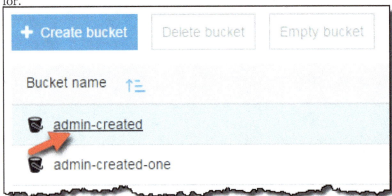

3. Choose **Properties**.

4. Choose **Static website hosting**.

After you enable your bucket for static website hosting, web browsers can access all of your content through the Amazon S3 website endpoint for your bucket.

Static website hosting   ✕

Endpoint : admin-created3.s3-website-us-west-2.amazonaws.com

○ Use this bucket to host

○ Redirect requests

5. Choose **Use this bucket to host**.

1. For **Index Document**, type the name of the index document, which is typically named `index.html`. When you configure a bucket for website hosting, you must specify an index document. Amazon S3 returns this index document when requests are made to the root domain or any of the subfolders. For more information, see Configure a Bucket for Website Hosting in the *Amazon Simple Storage Service Developer Guide*.

2. (Optional) For 4XX class errors, you can optionally provide your own custom error document that provides additional guidance for your users. For **Error Document**, type the name of the file that contains the custom error document. If an error occurs, Amazon S3 returns an HTML error document. For more information, see Custom Error Document Support in the *Amazon Simple Storage Service Developer Guide*.

3. (Optional) If you want to specify advanced redirection rules, in the **Edit redirection rules** text area, use XML to describe the rules. For example, you can conditionally route requests according to specific object key names or prefixes in the request. For more information, see Configure a Bucket for Website Hosting in the *Amazon Simple Storage Service Developer Guide*.

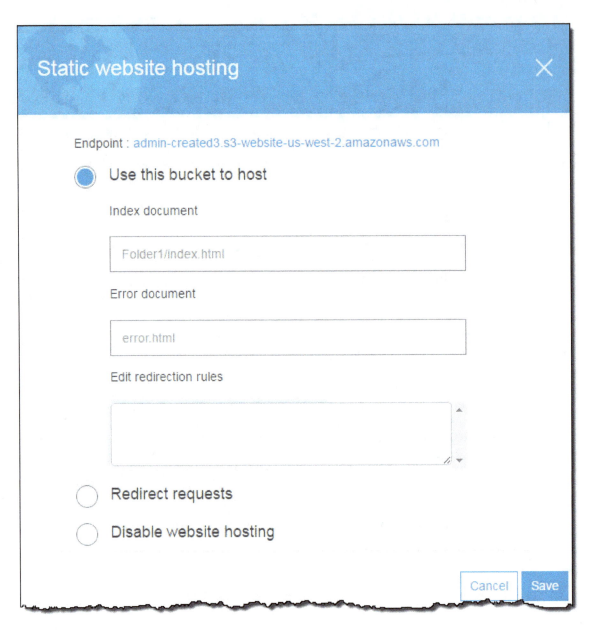

Static website hosting   ✕

Endpoint : admin-created3.s3-website-us-west-2.amazonaws.com

🔘 **Use this bucket to host**

Index document

Folder1/index.html

Error document

error.html

Edit redirection rules

⚪ **Redirect requests**

⚪ **Disable website hosting**

Cancel   **Save**

6. Choose **Save**.

7. Add a bucket policy to the website bucket that grants everyone access to the objects in the bucket. When you configure a bucket as a website, you must make the objects that you want to serve publicly readable. To do so, you write a bucket policy that grants everyone `s3:GetObject` permission. The following example bucket policy grants everyone access to the objects in the `example-bucket` bucket.

```
1  {
2      "Version": "2012-10-17",
3      "Statement": [
4          {
5              "Sid": "PublicReadGetObject",
6              "Effect": "Allow",
7              "Principal": "*",
8              "Action": [
9                  "s3:GetObject"
10             ],
11             "Resource": [
```

```
12                    "arn:aws:s3:::example-bucket/*"
13                ]
14            }
15        ]
16 }
```

For information about adding a bucket policy, see How Do I Add an S3 Bucket Policy?. For more information about website permissions, see Permissions Required for Website in the *Amazon Simple Storage Service Developer Guide.*

Note

If you choose **Disable website hosting**, Amazon S3 removes the website configuration from the bucket, so that the bucket is no longer accessible from the website endpoint. However, the bucket is still available at the REST endpoint. For a list of Amazon S3 endpoints, see Amazon S3 Regions and Endpoints in the *Amazon Web Services General Reference.*

How Do I Redirect Requests to an S3 Bucket Hosted Website to Another Host?

You can redirect all requests to your S3 bucket hosted static website to another host.

To redirect all requests to an S3 bucket's website endpoint to another host

1. Sign in to the AWS Management Console and open the Amazon S3 console at https://console.aws.amazon.com/s3/.

2. In the **Bucket name** list, choose the name of the bucket that you want to redirect all requests from.

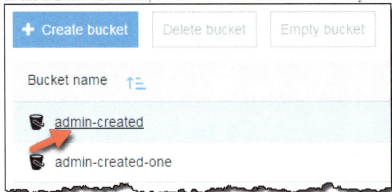

3. Choose **Properties**.

4. Choose **Static website hosting**.

5. Choose **Redirect requests**.

Static website hosting   ✕

Endpoint : admin-created3.s3-website-us-west-2.amazonaws.com

○ Use this bucket to host

● Redirect requests

Target Bucket or Domain

Bucketname1 or www.exampledomain.com

Protocol

https or http

○ Disable website hosting

Cancel   Save

1. For **Target bucket or domain**, type the name of the bucket or the domain name where you want requests to be redirected. To redirect requests to another bucket, type the name of the target bucket. For example, if you are redirecting to a root domain address, you would type **www.example.com**. For more information, see Configure a Bucket for Website Hosting in the *Amazon Simple Storage Service Developer Guide*.

2. For **Protocol**, type the protocol (http, https) for the redirected requests. If no protocol is specified, the protocol of the original request is used. If you redirect all requests, any request made to the bucket's website endpoint will be redirected to the specified host name.

6. Choose **Save**.

Advanced Settings for S3 Bucket Properties

This section describes how to configure advanced S3 bucket property settings for cross-region replication, event notification, and transfer acceleration.

How Do I Set Up a Destination to Receive Event Notifications?

Before you can enable event notifications for your bucket you must set up one of the following destination types:

An Amazon SNS topic

Amazon Simple Notification Service (Amazon SNS) is a web service that coordinates and manages the delivery or sending of messages to subscribing endpoints or clients. You can use the Amazon SNS console to create an Amazon SNS topic that your notifications can be sent to. The Amazon SNS topic must be in the same region as your Amazon S3 bucket. For information about creating an Amazon SNS topic, see Getting Started in the *Amazon Simple Notification Service Developer Guide*.

Before you can use the Amazon SNS topic that you create as an event notification destination, you need the following:

- The Amazon Resource Name (ARN) for the Amazon SNS topic

- A valid Amazon SNS topic subscription (the topic subscribers are notified when a message is published to your Amazon SNS topic)

- A permissions policy that you set up in the Amazon SNS console (as shown in the following example)

```
1  {
2    "Version":"2012-10-17",
3    "Id": "__example_policy_ID",
4    "Statement":[
5      {
6        "Sid": "example-statement-ID",
7        "Effect":"Allow",
8        "Principal": "*",
9        "Action": "SNS:Publish",
10       "Resource":"arn:aws:sns:region:account-number:topic-name",
11       "Condition": {
12         "ArnEquals": {
13           "aws:SourceArn": "arn:aws:s3:::bucket-name"
14         }
15       }
16     }
17   ]
18 }
```

An Amazon SQS queue

You can use the Amazon SQS console to create an Amazon SQS queue that your notifications can be sent to. The Amazon SQS queue must be in the same region as your Amazon S3 bucket. For information about creating an Amazon SQS queue, see Getting Started with Amazon SQS in the *Amazon Simple Queue Service Developer Guide*.

Before you can use the Amazon SQS queue as an event notification destination, you need the following:

- The Amazon Resource Name (ARN) for the Amazon SQS topic

- A permissions policy that you set up in the Amazon SQS console (as shown in the following example)

```
1  {
2    "Version":"2012-10-17",
3    "Id": "__example_policy_ID",
4    "Statement":[
5      {
6        "Sid": "example-statement-ID",
7        "Effect":"Allow",
8        "Principal": "*",
```

```
 9        "Action": "SQS:*",
10        "Resource":"arn:aws:sqs:region:account-number:queue-name",
11        "Condition": {
12          "ArnEquals": {
13           "aws:SourceArn": "arn:aws:s3:::bucket-name"
14          }
15        }
16      }
17    ]
18 }
```

A Lambda function

You can use the AWS Lambda console to create a Lambda function. The Lambda function must be in the same region as your S3 bucket. For information about creating a Lambda function, see the AWS Lambda Developer Guide.

Before you can use the Lambda function as an event notification destination, you must have the name or the ARN of a Lambda function to set up the Lambda function as a event notification destination.

For information about using Lambda with Amazon S3, see Using AWS Lambda: with Amazon S3 in the *AWS Lambda Developer Guide*.

How Do I Enable and Configure Event Notifications for an S3 Bucket?

You can enable certain Amazon S3 bucket events to send a notification message to a destination whenever the events occur. This section explains how to use the Amazon S3 console to enable event notifications. For more information about using event notifications , see Configuring Notifications for Amazon S3 Events in the *Amazon Simple Storage Service Developer Guide.*

Amazon S3 can send notifications for the following events:

- **An object created event** – You choose **ObjectCreated (All)** when configuring your events in the console to enable notifications for anytime an object is created in your bucket. Or, you can select one or more of the specific object-creation actions to trigger event notifications. These actions are **Put, Post, Copy**, and **CompleteMultiPartUpload**.

- **An object delete event** – You select **ObjectDelete (All)** when configuring your events in the console to enable notification for anytime an object is deleted. Or, you can select **Delete** to trigger event notifications when an unversioned object is deleted or a versioned object is permanently deleted. You select **Delete Marker Created** to trigger event notifications when a delete marker is created for a versioned object.

- **A Reduced Redundancy Storage (RRS) object lost event** – You select **RRSObjectLost** to be notified when Amazon S3 detects that an object of the RRS storage class has been lost.

Event notification messages can be sent to the following types of destinations:

- **An Amazon Simple Notification Service (Amazon SNS) topic** – A web service that coordinates and manages the delivery or sending of messages to subscribing endpoints or clients.

- **An Amazon Simple Queue Service (Amazon SQS) queue** – Offers reliable and scalable hosted queues for storing messages as they travel between computer.

- **A Lambda function** – AWS Lambda is a compute service where you can upload your code and the service can run the code on your behalf using the AWS infrastructure. You package up and upload your custom code to AWS Lambda when you create a Lambda function

Before you can enable event notifications for your bucket you must set up one of these destination types. For more information, see How Do I Set Up a Destination to Receive Event Notifications?.

To enable and configure event notifications for an S3 bucket

1. Sign in to the AWS Management Console and open the Amazon S3 console at https://console.aws.amazon.com/s3/.

2. In the **Bucket name** list, choose the name of the bucket that you want to enable events for.

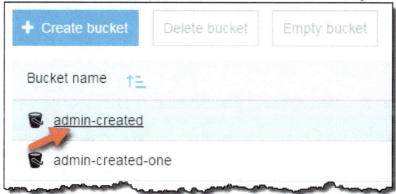

3. Choose **Properties**.

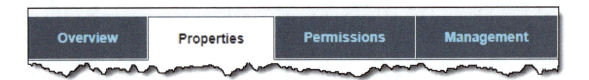

4. Under Advanced settings, choose **Events**.

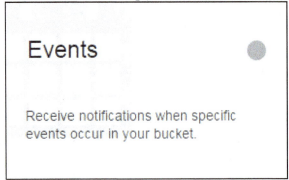

Events

Receive notifications when specific
events occur in your bucket.

5. Choose **Add notification**.

Events   ×

+ Add notification   Delete   Edit

Name	Events	Filter	Type

Cancel   Save

6. In **Name**, type a descriptive name for your event configuration. If you do not enter a name, a GUID is autogenerated and used for the name.

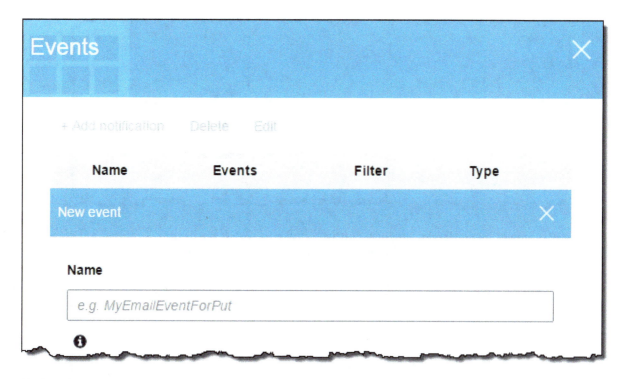

7. Under **Events**, select one or more of the type of event occurrences that you want to receive notifications for. When the event occurs a notification is sent to a destination that you choose. For example, you could do any of the following:

- Select **ObjectCreate (All)** to enable event notifications for anytime an object is created in the bucket.

- Select **Put** and **Complete MultipartUpload** to trigger event notifications anytime a new object is put into a bucket and anytime a multipart upload completes.

- Select **ObjectDelete (All)** to enable event notifications for anytime an object is deleted in the bucket.

- Select **Delete** or **Delete Marker Created** to trigger notifications for specific types of object deletes.

For information about deleting versioned objects, see Deleting Object Versions. For information about object versioning, see Object Versioning and Using Versioning. **Note**
When you delete the last object from a folder Amazon S3 can generate an object creation event. The Amazon S3 console displays a folder under the following circumstances: 1) when a zero byte object has a trailing slash (/) in its name (in this case there is an actual Amazon S3 object of 0 bytes that represents a folder), and 2) if the object has a slash (/) within its name (in this case there isn't an actual object representing the folder). When there are multiple objects with the same prefix with a trailing slash (/) as part of their names, those objects are shown as being part of a folder. The name of the folder is formed from the characters preceding the trailing slash (/). When you delete all the objects listed under that folder, there is no actual object available to represent the empty folder. Under such circumstance the Amazon S3 console creates a zero byte object to represent that folder. If you enabled event notification for creation of objects, the zero byte object creation action that is taken by the console will trigger an object creation event.

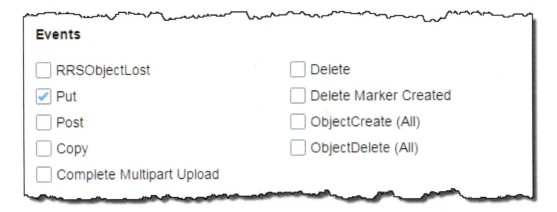

8. Type an object name **Prefix** and/or a **Suffix** to filter the event notifications by the prefix and/or suffix. For example, you can set up a filter so that you are sent a notification only when files are added to an image folder (for example, objects with the name prefix `images/`). For more information, see Configuring Notifications with Object Key Name Filtering.

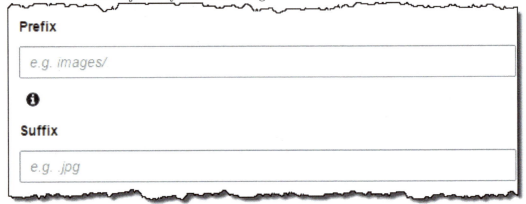

9. Select the type of destination to have the event notifications sent to.

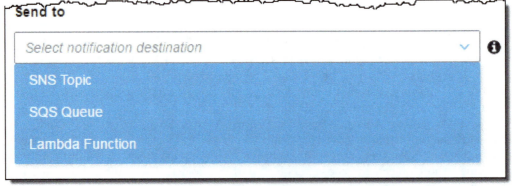

1. If you select the **SNS Topic** destination type.

   1. In the **SNS topic** box, type the name or select from the menu, the Amazon SNS topic that will receive notifications from Amazon S3. For information about the Amazon SNS topic format, see SNS FAQ.

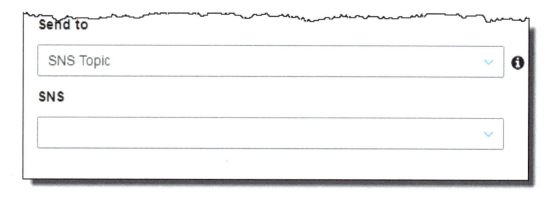

2. (Optional) You can also select **Add SNS topic ARN** from the menu and type the **ARN** of the SNS topic in **SNS topic ARN**.

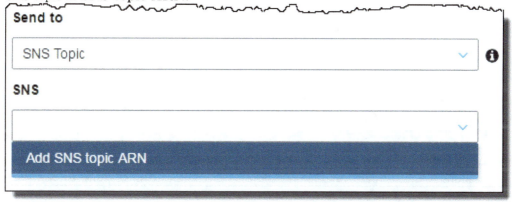

2. If you select the **SQS queue** destination type, do the following:

    1. In **SQS queue**, type or choose a name from the menu of the Amazon SQS queue that you want to receive notifications from Amazon S3. For information about Amazon SQS, see What is Amazon Simple Queue Service? in the *Amazon Simple Queue Service Developer Guide*.

    2. (Optional) You can also select **Add SQS topic ARN** from the menu and type the ARN of the SQS queue in **SQS queue ARN**.

3. If you select the **Lambda Function** destination type, do the following:

    1. In **Lambda Function**, type or choose the name of the Lambda function that you want to receive notifications from Amazon S3.

    2. If you don't have any Lambda functions in the region that contains your bucket, you'll be prompted to enter a Lambda function ARN. In **Lambda Function ARN**, type the ARN of the Lambda function that you want to receive notifications from Amazon S3.

    3. (Optional) You can also choose **Add Lambda function ARN** from the menu and type the ARN of the Lambda function in **Lambda function ARN**.

    For information about using Lambda with Amazon S3, see Using AWS Lambda: with Amazon S3 in the *AWS Lambda Developer Guide*.

10. Choose **Save**. Amazon S3 will send a test message to the event notification destination.

How Do I Enable Transfer Acceleration for an S3 Bucket?

Amazon Simple Storage Service (Amazon S3) transfer acceleration enables fast, easy, and secure transfers of files between your client and an S3 bucket over long distances. This topic describes how to enable Amazon S3 transfer acceleration for a bucket. For more information, see Amazon S3 Transfer Acceleration in the *Amazon Simple Storage Service Developer Guide*.

To enable transfer acceleration for an S3 bucket

1. Sign in to the AWS Management Console and open the Amazon S3 console at https://console.aws.amazon.com/s3/.

2. In the **Bucket name** list, choose the name of the bucket that you want to enable transfer acceleration for.

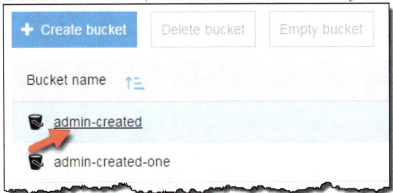

3. Choose **Properties**.

4. Choose **Transfer acceleration**.

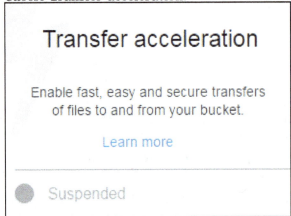

5. Choose **Enabled**, and then choose **Save**.

   Endpoint displays the endpoint domain name that you use to access accelerated data transfers to and from the bucket that is enabled for transfer acceleration. If you suspend transfer acceleration, the accelerate endpoint no longer works.

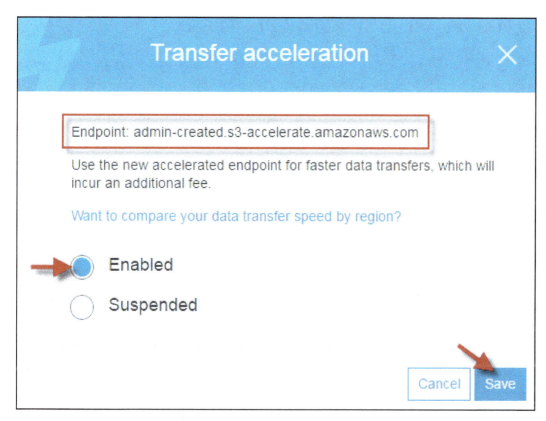

6. (Optional) If you want to run the Amazon S3 Transfer Acceleration Speed Comparison tool, which compares accelerated and non-accelerated upload speeds starting with the Region in which the transfer acceleration bucket is enabled, choose the **Want to compare your data transfer speed by region?** option. The Speed Comparison tool uses multipart uploads to transfer a file from your browser to various AWS Regions with and without using Amazon S3 transfer acceleration.

More Info
How Do I View the Properties for an S3 Bucket?

Uploading, Downloading, and Managing Objects

Amazon S3 is cloud storage for the Internet. To upload your data (photos, videos, documents etc.), you first create a bucket in one of the AWS Regions. You can then upload an unlimited number of data objects to the bucket.

The data that you store in Amazon S3 consists of objects. Every object resides within a bucket that you create in a specific AWS Region. Every object that you store in Amazon S3 resides in a bucket.

Objects stored in a region never leave the region unless you explicitly transfer them to another region. For example, objects stored in the EU (Ireland) region never leave it. The objects stored in an AWS region physically remain in that region. Amazon S3 does not keep copies of objects or move them to any other region. However, you can access the objects from anywhere, as long as you have necessary permissions to do so.

Before you can upload an object into Amazon S3, you must have write permissions to a bucket.

Objects can be any file type: images, backups, data, movies, etc. The maximum size of file you can upload by using the Amazon S3 console is 78GB. You can have an unlimited number of objects in a bucket.

The following topics explain how to use the Amazon S3 console to upload, delete, and manage objects.

How Do I Upload Files and Folders to an S3 Bucket?

This topic explains how to use the AWS Management Console to upload one or more files or entire folders to an Amazon S3 bucket. Before you can upload files and folders to an Amazon S3 bucket, you need write permissions for the bucket. For more information about access permissions, see Setting Bucket and Object Access Permissions.

When you upload a file to Amazon S3, it is stored as an S3 object. Objects consist of the file data and metadata that describes the object. You can have an unlimited number of objects in a bucket.

You can upload any file type—images, backups, data, movies, etc—into an S3 bucket. The maximum size of a file that you can upload by using the Amazon S3 console is 78 GB.

You can upload files by dragging and dropping or by pointing and clicking. To upload folders, you *must* drag and drop them. Drag and drop functionality is supported *only* for the Chrome and Firefox browsers. For information about which Chrome and Firefox browser versions are supported, see Which Browsers are Supported for Use with the AWS Management Console?.

When you upload a folder, Amazon S3 uploads all of the files and subfolders from the specified folder to your bucket. It then assigns an object key name that is a combination of the uploaded file name and the folder name. For example, if you upload a folder called `/images` that contains two files, `sample1.jpg` and `sample2.jpg`, Amazon S3 uploads the files and then assigns the corresponding key names, `images/sample1.jpg` and `images/sample2.jpg`. The key names include the folder name as a prefix. The Amazon S3 console displays only the part of the key name that follows the last "/". For example, within an images folder the `images/sample1.jpg` and `images/sample2.jpg` objects are displayed as `sample1.jpg` and a `sample2.jpg`.

If you upload individual files and you have a folder open in the Amazon S3 console, when Amazon S3 uploads the files, it includes the name of the open folder as the prefix of the key names. For example, if you have a folder named `backup` open in the Amazon S3 console and you upload a file named `sample1.jpg`, the key name is `backup/sample1.jpg`. However, the object is displayed in the console as `sample1.jpg` in the `backup` folder.

If you upload individual files and you do not have a folder open in the Amazon S3 console, when Amazon S3 uploads the files, it assigns only the file name as the key name. For example, if you upload a file named `sample1.jpg`, the key name is `sample1.jpg`. For more information on key names, see Object Key and Metadata in the *Amazon Simple Storage Service Developer Guide*.

If you upload an object with a key name that already exists in a versioning-enabled bucket, Amazon S3 creates another version of the object instead of replacing the existing object. For more information about versioning, see How Do I Enable or Suspend Versioning for an S3 Bucket?.

Uploading Files and Folders by Using Drag and Drop

If you are using the Chrome or Firefox browsers, you can choose the folders and files to upload, and then drag and drop them into the destination bucket. Dragging and dropping is the *only* way that you can upload folders.

To upload folders and files to an S3 bucket by using drag and drop

1. Sign in to the AWS Management Console and open the Amazon S3 console at https://console.aws.amazon.com/s3/.

2. In the **Bucket name** list, choose the name of the bucket that you want to upload your folders or files to.

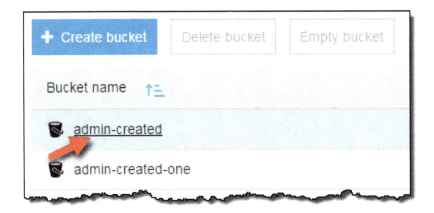

3. Drag and drop your selections into the console window that lists the objects in the destination bucket.

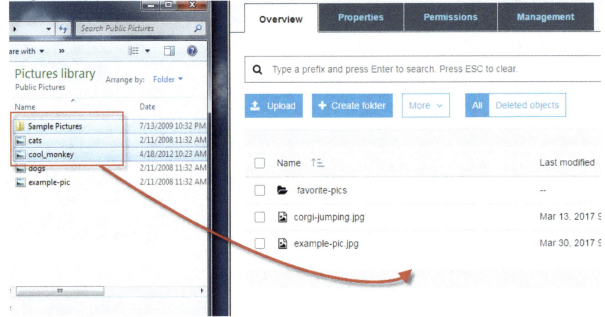

The files you chose are listed in the **Upload** dialog box.

4. In the **Upload** dialog box, do one of the following:

   1. Drag and drop more files and folders to the console window that displays the **Upload** dialog box. To add more files, you can also choose **Add more files**. This option works *only* for files, not folders.

   2. To immediately upload the listed files and folders without granting or removing permissions for specific users or setting public permissions for all of the files that you're uploading, choose **Upload**. For information about object access permissions, see How Do I Set Permissions on an Object?.

   3. To set permissions or properties for the files that you are uploading, choose **Next**.

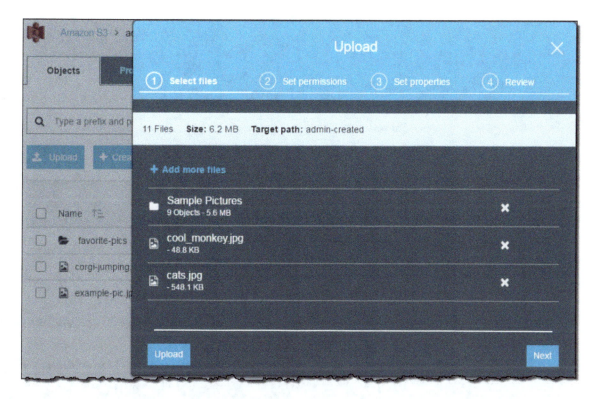

5. On the **Set Permissions** page, under **Manage users** you can change the permissions for the AWS account owner. The *owner* refers to the AWS account root user, and not an AWS Identity and Access Management (IAM) user. For more information about the root user, see The AWS Account Root User.

Under **Manage public permissions** you can grant read access to your objects to the general public (everyone in the world), for all of the files that you're uploading. Granting public read access is applicable to a small subset of use cases such as when buckets are used for websites. We recommend that you do not change the default setting of **Do not grant public read access to this object(s)**. You can always make changes to object permissions after you upload the object. For information about object access permissions, see How Do I Set Permissions on an Object?.

When you're done configuring permissions, choose **Next**.

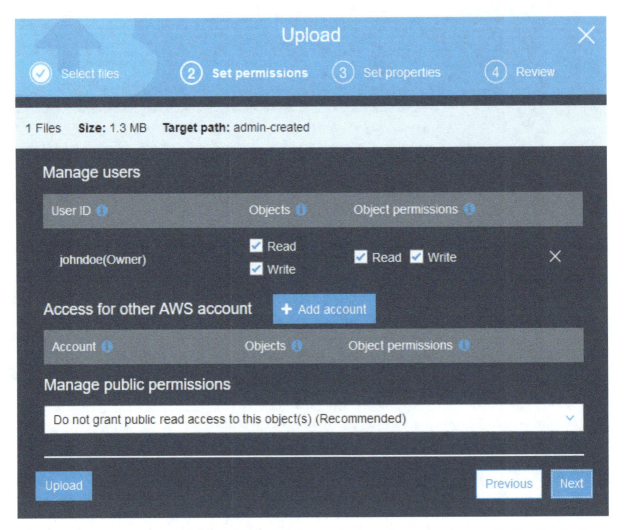

6. On the **Set Properties** page, choose the storage class and encryption method to use for the files that you are uploading. You can also add or modify metadata.

   1. Choose a storage class for the files you're uploading. For more information about storage classes, see Storage Classes in the *Amazon Simple Storage Service Developer Guide*.

   2. Choose the type of encryption for the files that you're uploading. If you don't want to encrypt them, choose **None**.

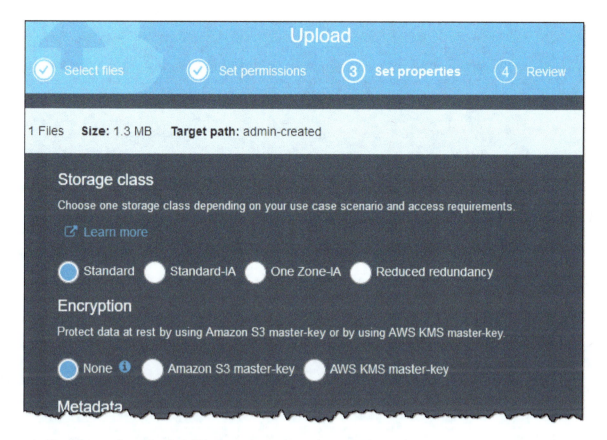

1. To encrypt the uploaded files using keys that are managed by Amazon S3, choose **Amazon S3 master-key**. For more information, see Protecting Data with Amazon S3-Managed Encryption Keys Classes in the *Amazon Simple Storage Service Developer Guide.*

2. To encrypt the uploaded files using the AWS Key Management Service (AWS KMS), choose **AWS KMS master-key**. Then choose a master key from the list of AWS KMS master keys. **Note**
   To encrypt objects in a bucket, you can use only keys that are available in the same AWS Region as the bucket.

   You can give an external account the ability to use an object that is protected by an AWS KMS key. To do this, select **Custom KMS ARN** from the list and enter the Amazon Resource Name (ARN) for the external account. Administrators of an external account that have usage permissions to an object protected by your AWS KMS key can further restrict access by creating a resource-level IAM policy.

   For more information about creating an AWS KMS key, see Creating Keys in the *AWS Key Management Service Developer Guide.* For more information about protecting data with AWS KMS, see Protecting Data with AWS KMS–Managed Key in the *Amazon Simple Storage Service Developer Guide.*

3. If you want to add Amazon S3 system-defined metadata to all of the objects you are uploading, for **Header**, select a header. You can select common HTTP headers, such as **Content-Type** and **Content-Disposition**. Type a value for the header, and then choose **Save**. For a list of system-defined metadata and information about whether you can add the value, see System-Defined Metadata in the *Amazon Simple Storage Service Developer Guide.*

4. To add user-defined metadata to all of the objects that you are uploading, type `x-amz-meta-` plus a custom metadata name in the **Header** field. Type a value for the header, and then choose **Save**. For more information about user-defined metadata, see User-Defined Metadata in the *Amazon Simple Storage Service Developer Guide.*

Metadata for Amazon S3 objects is represented by a name-value (key-value) pair. User-defined metadata is stored with the object, and is returned when you download the object. User-defined metadata can be as large as 2 KB. Both the keys and their values must conform to US-ASCII standards. Any metadata starting with prefix `x-amz-meta-` is treated as user-defined metadata. Amazon S3 does not process user-defined metadata.

7. Choose **Next**.

8. On the **Upload** review page, verify that your settings are correct, and then choose **Upload**. To make changes, choose **Previous**.

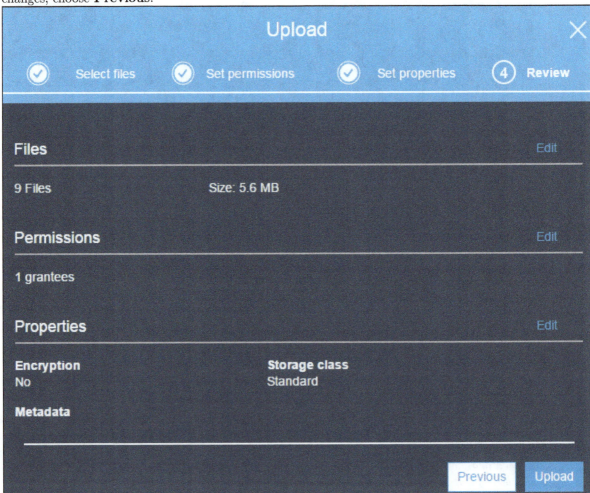

9. To see the progress of the upload, choose **In progress** at the bottom of the browser window.

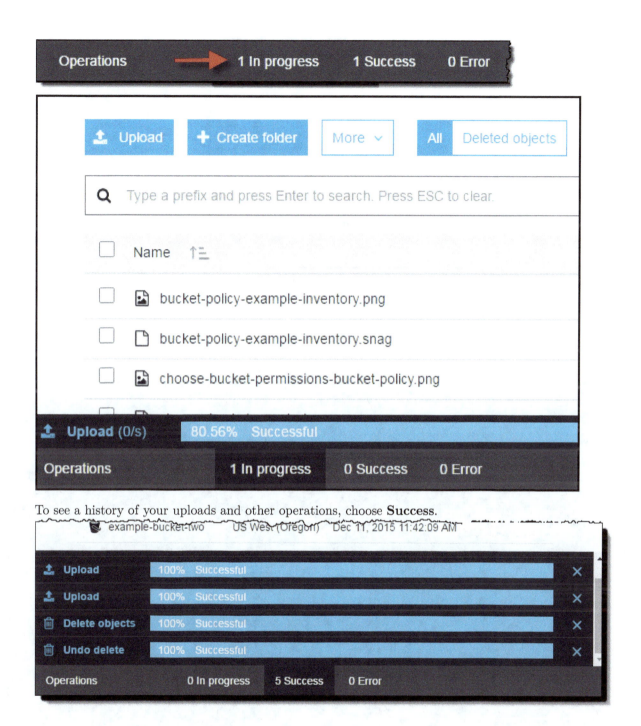

To see a history of your uploads and other operations, choose **Success**.

Uploading Files by Pointing and Clicking

This procedure explains how to upload files into an S3 bucket by choosing **Upload**.

To upload files to an S3 bucket by pointing and clicking

1. Sign in to the AWS Management Console and open the Amazon S3 console at https://console.aws.amazon.com/s3/.

2. In the **Bucket name** list, choose the name of the bucket that you want to upload your files to.

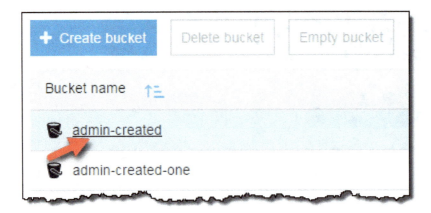

3. Choose **Upload**.

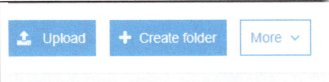

4. In the **Upload** dialog box, choose **Add files**.

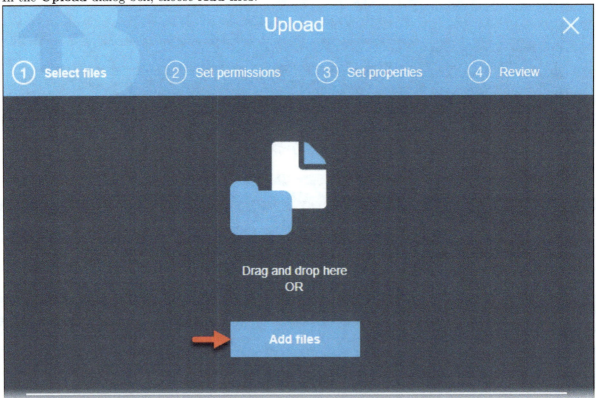

5. Choose one or more files to upload, and then choose **Open.**

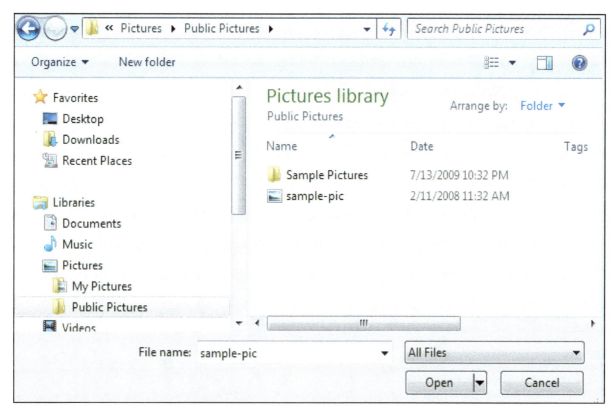

6. After you see the files that you chose listed in the **Upload** dialog box, do one of the following:

   1. To add more files, choose **Add more files**.

   2. To immediately upload the listed files, choose **Upload**.

   3. To set permissions or properties for the files that you are uploading, choose **Next**.

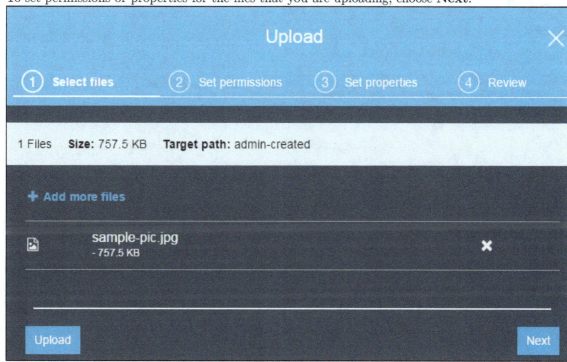

7. To set permissions and properties, start with **Step 5** of Uploading Files and Folders by Using Drag and

Drop.

More Info

- How Do I Set Permissions on an Object?.
- How Do I Download an Object from an S3 Bucket?

How Do I Download an Object from an S3 Bucket?

This section explains how to use the Amazon S3 console to download objects from an S3 bucket.

Data transfer fees apply when you download objects. For information about Amazon S3 features, and pricing, see Amazon S3.

To download an object from an S3 bucket

1. Sign in to the AWS Management Console and open the Amazon S3 console at https://console.aws.amazon.com/s3/.

2. In the **Bucket name** list, choose the name of the bucket that you want to download an object from.

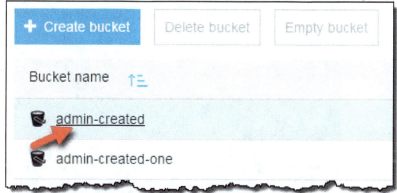

3. You can download an object from an S3 bucket in any of the following ways:

   - In the **Name** list, select the check box next to the object you want to download, and then choose **Download** on the object description page that appears.

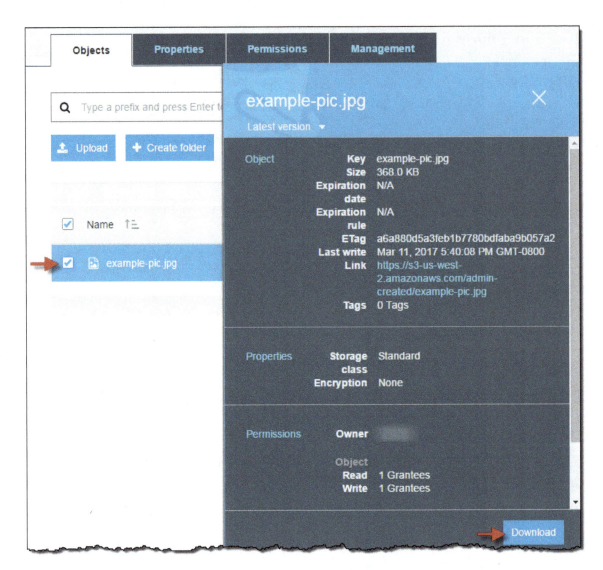

- Choose the name of the object that you want to download.

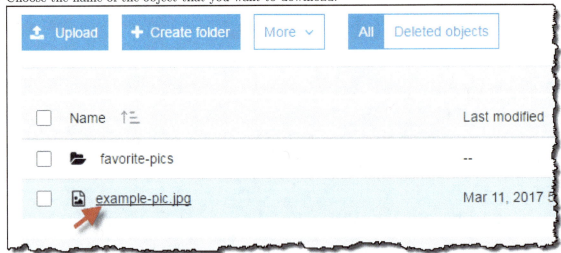

On the **Overview** page, choose **Download**.

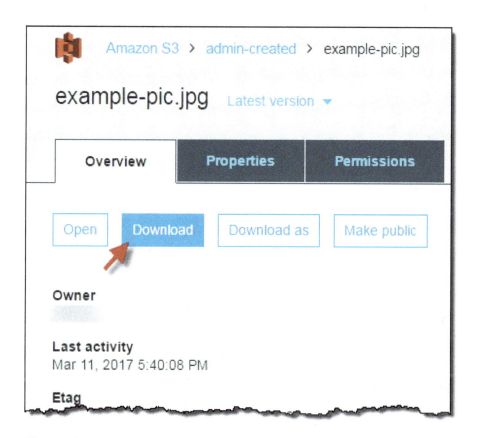

- Choose the name of the object that you want to download and then choose **Download as** on the **Overview** page.

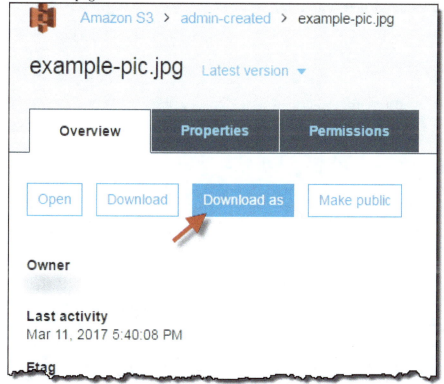

- Choose the name of the object that you want to download. Choose **Latest version** and then choose the download icon.

Related Topics

- How Do I Upload Files and Folders to an S3 Bucket?

How Do I Delete Objects from an S3 Bucket?

This section explains how to use the Amazon S3 console to delete objects. Because all objects in your S3 bucket incur storage costs, you should delete objects that you no longer need. If you are collecting log files, for example, it's a good idea to delete them when they're no longer needed. You can set up a lifecycle rule to automatically delete objects such as log files.

For information about Amazon S3 features and pricing, see Amazon S3.

To delete objects from an S3 bucket

1. Sign in to the AWS Management Console and open the Amazon S3 console at https://console.aws.amazon. com/s3/.

2. In the **Bucket name** list, choose the name of the bucket that you want to delete an object from.

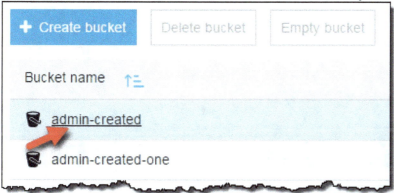

3. You can delete objects from an S3 bucket in any of the following ways:

   - In the **Name** list, select the check box next to the objects and folders that you want to delete, choose **More**, and then choose **Delete**.

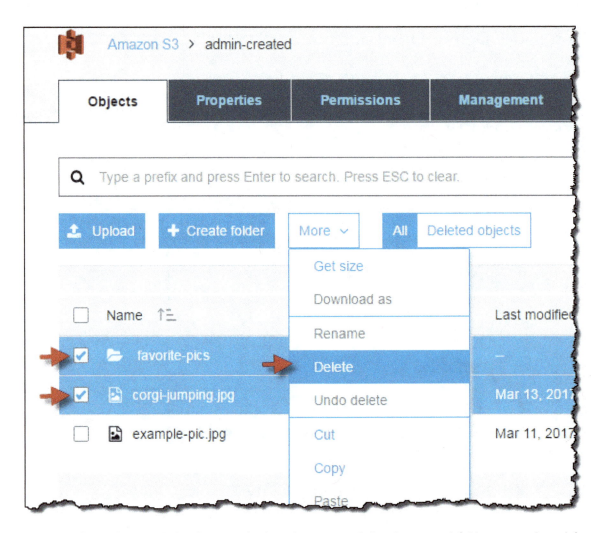

In the **Delete objects** dialog box, verify that the names of the objects and folders you selected for deletion are listed and then choose **Delete**.

- Choose the name of the object that you want to delete, choose **Latest version**, and then choose the trash can icon.

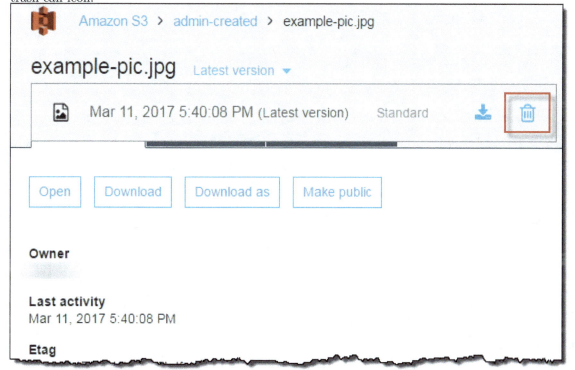

More Info

- How Do I Undelete a Deleted S3 Object?
- How Do I Create a Lifecycle Policy for an S3 Bucket?

How Do I Undelete a Deleted S3 Object?

This section explains how to use the Amazon S3 console to recover (undelete) deleted objects.

To be able to undelete a deleted object, you must have had versioning enabled on the bucket that contains the object before the object was deleted. For information about enabling versioning, see How Do I Enable or Suspend Versioning for an S3 Bucket?.

When you delete an object in a versioning-enabled bucket, all versions remain in the bucket and Amazon S3 creates a delete marker for the object. To undelete the object, you must delete this delete marker. For more information about versioning and delete markers, see Object Versioning in the *Amazon Simple Storage Service Developer Guide*.

To recover deleted objects from an S3 bucket

1. Sign in to the AWS Management Console and open the Amazon S3 console at https://console.aws.amazon.com/s3/.

2. In the **Bucket name** list, choose the name of the bucket that you want.

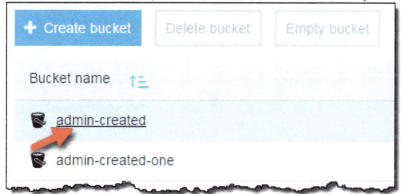

3. To see a list of the versions of the objects in the bucket, choose **Show**. You'll be able to see the delete markers for deleted objects.

4. To undelete an object, you must delete the delete marker. Select the check box next to the delete marker of the object to recover, and then choose **delete** from the **More** menu.

Name	Version ID
amazon-reindeer.jpg	
☐ 🖼 Sep 1, 2017 5:43:05 PM (Latest version)	na_axXxRr.xXDaWfcp4idCkIpXsyv6m9
☐ 🖼 Sep 1, 2017 5:42:50 PM	cM5IuTOwME0WUDRZuAqv7vbhm7Zi...
amazon-spheres.jpg	
☑ 🖼 Sep 1, 2017 5:46:31 PM (Delete marker)	XfdtMN.2X.yHhbNIceyAoM_mIkDA3Nzi
☐ 🖼 Sep 1, 2017 5:43:07 PM	1yAY8OBXQoaELJ0L393xCg.CqjbGe...
☐ 🖼 Sep 1, 2017 5:42:52 PM	Ai4hSgfCIjB902ygpjQErUQPbVj7HMur
screen-shot3.png	
☐ 🖼 Apr 15, 2016 4:04:18 PM (Latest version)	null

5. Choose **Hide**, you'll see the undeleted object listed.

More Info

- How Do I See the Versions of an S3 Object?
- How Do I Enable or Suspend Versioning for an S3 Bucket?
- Using Versioning in the *Amazon Simple Storage Service Developer Guide*

How Do I Delete Folders from an S3 Bucket?

This section explains how to use the Amazon S3 console to delete folders from an S3 bucket.

For information about Amazon S3 features and pricing, see Amazon S3.

To delete folders from an S3 bucket

1. Sign in to the AWS Management Console and open the Amazon S3 console at https://console.aws.amazon.com/s3/.

2. In the **Bucket name** list, choose the name of the bucket that you want to delete folders from.

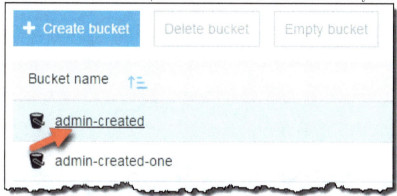

3. In the **Name** list, select the check box next to the folders and objects that you want to delete, choose **More**, and then choose **Delete**.

67

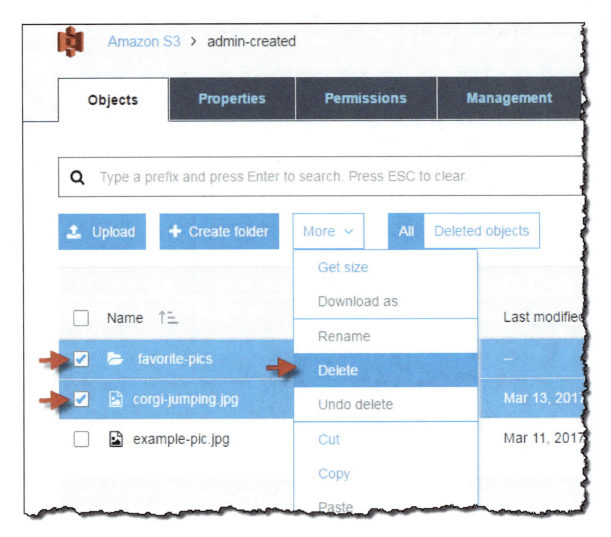

In the **Delete objects** dialog box, verify that the names of the folders you selected for deletion are listed and then choose **Delete**.

Related Topics

- How Do I Delete Objects from an S3 Bucket?

How Do I Restore an S3 Object That Has Been Archived to Amazon Glacier?

This section explains how to use the Amazon S3 console to restore an object that has been archived by using the `Glacier` storage class. Objects in the `Glacier` storage class are not immediately accessible. To access an object in this class, you must restore a temporary copy of it to its S3 bucket. You can access objects that have been archived to Amazon Glacier only by using Amazon S3. You can't use the Amazon Glacier console, AWS command line interface (CLI), or APIs to see the S3 archived objects. For information about when to use the `Glacier` storage class for objects, see Storage Classes and Object Lifecycle Management in the *Amazon Simple Storage Service Developer Guide*.

Amazon Glacier charges a retrieval fee for retrieving objects stored with the `Glacier` storage class. For retrieval pricing information, see Amazon Glacier Pricing.

When you restore an archive, you pay for both the archive and the restored copy. Because there is a storage cost for the copy, restore objects only for the duration you need them. If you want a permanent copy of the object, create a copy of it in your S3 bucket. For information about Amazon S3 features and pricing, see Amazon S3.

After restoring an object, you can download it from the **Overview** page. For more information, see How Do I See an Overview of an Object?.

Archive Retrieval Options

You restore archived objects using one of the following retrieval types:

- **Expedited retrieval** – Expedited retrievals typically retrieve objects within 1–5 minutes. There are two types of Expedited retrievals: On-Demand and Provisioned.
  - **On-Demand** – If you don't need a guarantee that your expedited retrieval requests will be immediately successful, and you don't want to purchase provisioned capacity, use On-Demand expedited retrievals. Amazon S3 processes On-Demand expedited retrieval requests the vast majority of the time. It fails to process them only in rare situations where there is an unusually high retrieval demand. In that case, repeat the request.
  - **Provisioned** – If you need to guarantee that your expedited retrieval requests are processed immediately and you have or are willing to purchase provisioned capacity, use Provisioned expedited retrievals. After purchasing provisioned capacity, all of your expedited retrievals are served by this capacity. For pricing information on provisioned capacity, see Amazon Glacier Pricing.
- **Standard retrieval** – Standard retrievals allow you to access your archived objects within several hours,. typically within 3–5 hours.
- **Bulk retrieval** – Bulk retrievals are Amazon Glacier's lowest-cost retrieval option. With bulk retrieval, you can retrieve large amounts, even petabytes, of data inexpensively in a day. Bulk retrievals typically are complete within 5–12 hours.

For more information about retrieval options, see Restoring Archived Objects in the *Amazon Simple Storage Service Developer Guide*.

Restoring an Archived S3 Object

This topic explains how to use the Amazon S3 console to restore an object that has been archived to Amazon Glacier.

To restore archived S3 objects

1. Sign in to the AWS Management Console and open the Amazon S3 console at https://console.aws.amazon.com/s3/.

2. In the **Bucket name** list, choose the name of the bucket that contains the objects that you want to restore.

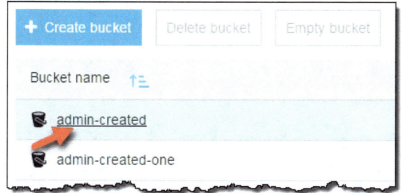

3. In the **Name** list, select the objects that you want to restore, choose **More**, and then choose **Initiate restore**.

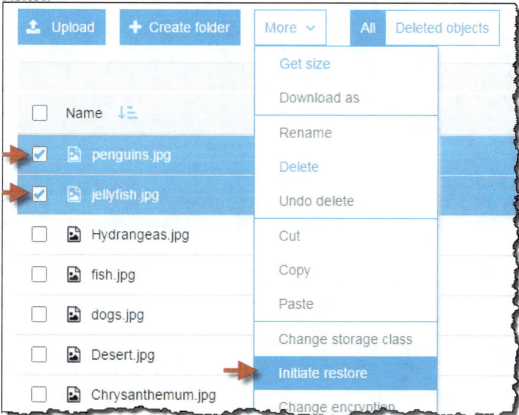

4. In the **Initiate restore** dialog box, type the number of days that you want your archived data to be accessible.

5. Choose one of the following retrieval options from the **Retrieval options** menu.

   • Choose **Bulk retrieval** or **Standard retrieval**, and then choose **Restore**.

   • Choose **Expedited retrieval**.

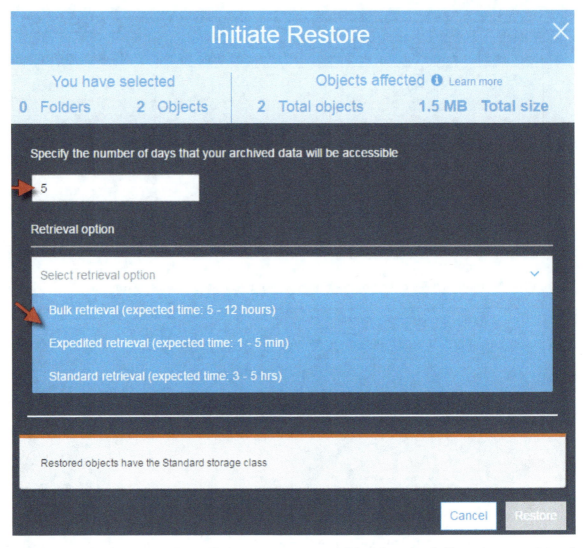

6. If you have provisioned capacity, choose **Restore** to start a provisioned retrieval. If you have provisioned capacity, all of your expedited retrievals are served by your provisioned capacity. For more information about provisioned capacity, see Archive Retrieval Options.

- If you don't have provisioned capacity and you don't want to buy it, choose **Restore** to start an On-Demand retrieval.

- If you don't have provisioned capacity, but you want to buy it, choose **Add capacity unit**, and then choose **Buy**. When you get the **Purchase succeeded** message, choose **Restore** to start provisioned retrieval.

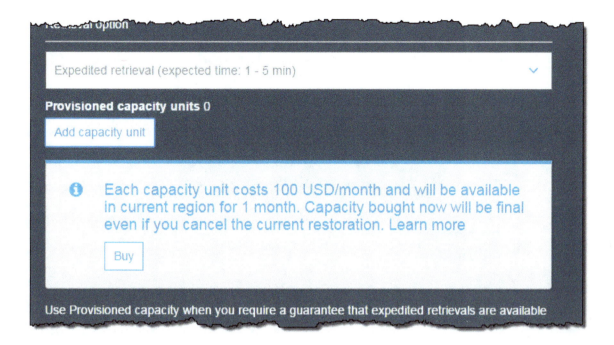

Checking Archive Upload Status and Expiration Date

To check the progress of the restoration, see the object overview panel. For information about the overview panel, see How Do I See an Overview of an Object?.

The **Properties** section shows that restoration is **In progress**.

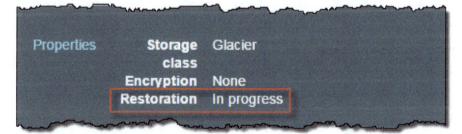

When the temporary copy of the object is available, the object's **Properties** section shows the **Restoration expiry date**. This is when Amazon S3 will remove the restored copy of your archive.

Restored objects are stored only for the number of days that you specify. If you want a permanent copy of the object, create a copy of it in your Amazon S3 bucket.

Amazon S3 calculates the expiry date by adding the number of days that you specify to the time you request to restore the object, and then rounding to the next day at midnight UTC. This calculation applies to the initial restoration of the object and to any extensions to availability that you request. For example, if an object was restored on 10/15/2012 10:30 AM UTC and the number of days that you specified is 3, then the object is available until 10/19/2012 00:00 UTC. If, on 10/16/2012 11:00 AM UTC you change the number of days that you want it to be accessible to 1, then Amazon S3 makes the restored object available until 10/18/2012 00:00 UTC.

After restoring an object, you can download it from the **Overview** page. For more information, see How Do I See an Overview of an Object?.

More Info

- How Do I Create a Lifecycle Policy for an S3 Bucket?
- How Do I Undelete a Deleted S3 Object?

How Do I See an Overview of an Object?

This section explains how to use the Amazon S3 console to view the object overview panel. This panel provides an overview of all the essential information for an object in one place.

To see the overview panel for an object

1. Sign in to the AWS Management Console and open the Amazon S3 console at https://console.aws.amazon.com/s3/.

2. In the **Bucket name** list, choose the name of the bucket that contains the object.

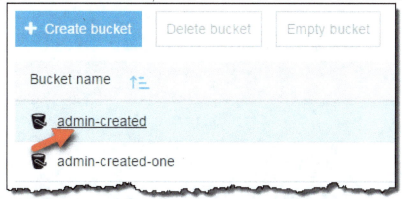

3. In the **Name** list, select the check box next to the name of the object for which you want an overview.

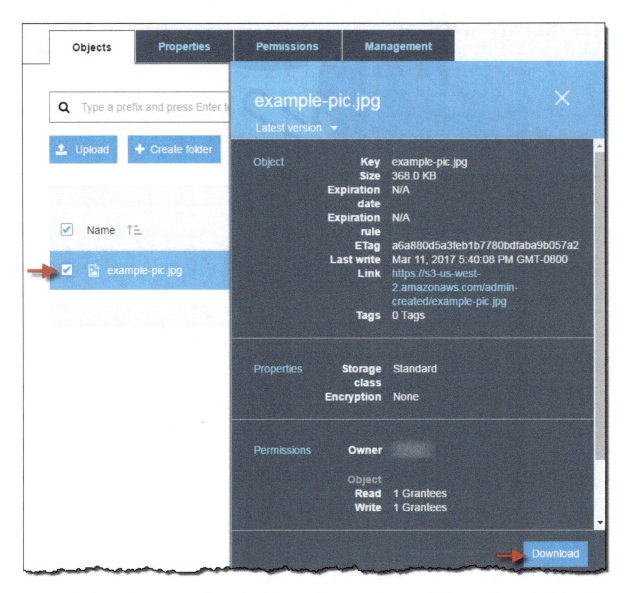

4. To download the object, choose **Download** in the object overview panel. To copy the path of the object to the clipboard, choose **Copy Path**.

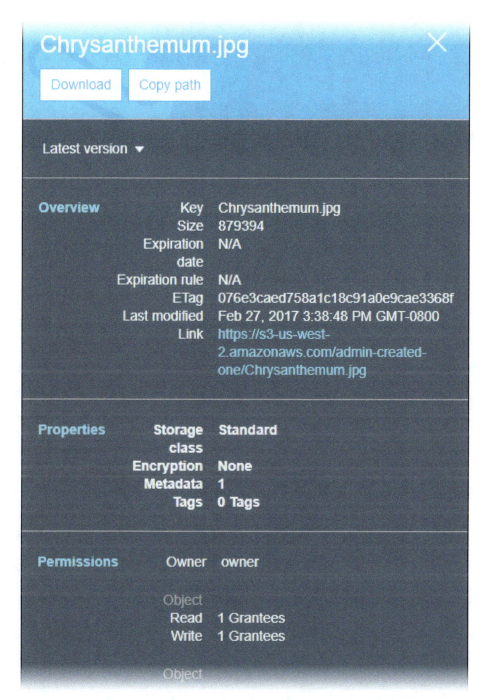

5. If versioning is enabled on the bucket, choose **Latest versions** to list the versions of the object. You can then choose the download icon to download an object version, or choose the trash can icon to delete an object version.

Important

You can undelete an object only if it was deleted as the latest (current) version. You can't undelete a previous version of an object that was deleted. For more information, see Object Versioning and Using Versioning in the *Amazon Simple Storage Service Developer Guide*.

More Info

- How Do I See the Versions of an S3 Object?

How Do I See the Versions of an S3 Object?

This section explains how to use the Amazon S3 console to see the different versions of an object.

A versioning-enabled bucket can have many versions of the same object:, one current (latest) version and zero or more noncurrent (previous) versions. Amazon S3 assigns each object a unique version ID. For information about enabling versioning, see How Do I Enable or Suspend Versioning for an S3 Bucket?.

If a bucket is versioning-enabled, Amazon S3 creates another version of an object under the following conditions:

- If you upload an object that has the same name as an object that already exists in the bucket, Amazon S3 creates another version of the object instead of replacing the existing object.

- If you update any object properties after you upload the object to the bucket, such as changing the storage details or other metadata , Amazon S3 creates a new object version in the bucket.

For more information about versioning support in Amazon S3, see Object Versioning and Using Versioning in the *Amazon Simple Storage Service Developer Guide*.

To see multiple versions of an object

1. Sign in to the AWS Management Console and open the Amazon S3 console at https://console.aws.amazon. com/s3/.

2. In the **Bucket name** list, choose the name of the bucket that contains the object.

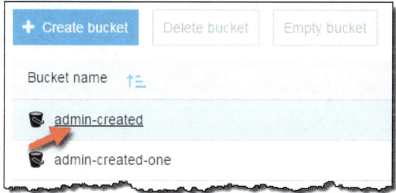

3. To see a list of the versions of the objects in the bucket, choose **Show**. For each object version, the console shows a unique version ID, the date and time the object version was created, and other properties. (Objects stored in your bucket before you set the versioning state have a version ID of **null**.)

   To list the objects without the versions, choose **Hide**.

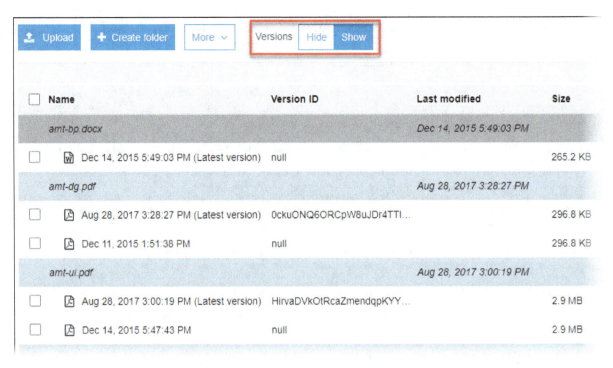

You also can view, download, and delete object versions in the object overview panel. For more information, see How Do I See an Overview of an Object?.

Important
You can undelete an object only if it was deleted as the latest (current) version. You can't undelete a previous version of an object that was deleted. For more information, see Object Versioning and Using Versioning in the *Amazon Simple Storage Service Developer Guide*.

More Info

- How Do I Enable or Suspend Versioning for an S3 Bucket?
- How Do I Create a Lifecycle Policy for an S3 Bucket?

How Do I View the Properties of an Object?

This section explains how to use the console to view the properties of an object.

To view the properties of an object

1. Sign in to the AWS Management Console and open the Amazon S3 console at https://console.aws.amazon.com/s3/.

2. In the **Bucket name** list, choose the name of the bucket that contains the object.

3. In the **Name** list, choose the name of the object you want to view the properties for.

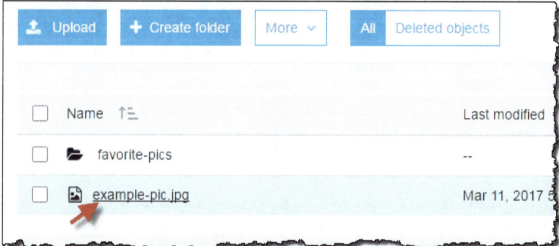

4. Choose **Properties**.

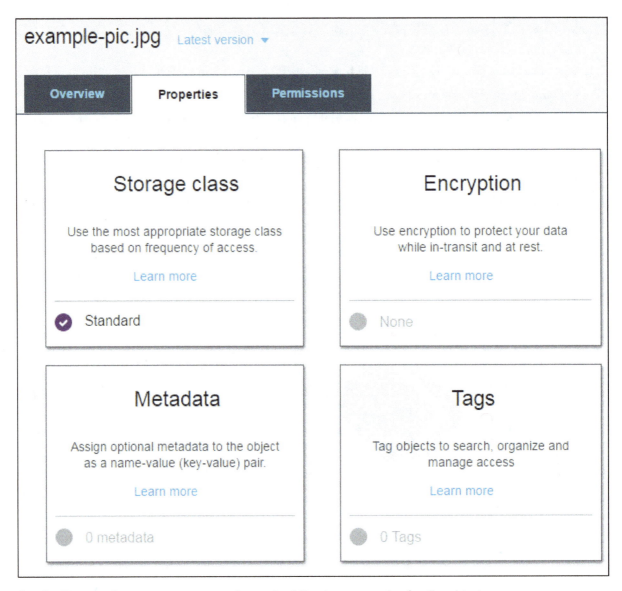

5. On the **Properties** page, you can configure the following properties for the object.

   1. **Storage class** – Each object in Amazon S3 has a storage class associated with it. The storage class that you choose to use depends on how frequently you access the object. The default storage class for S3 objects is STANDARD. You choose which storage class to use when you upload an object. For more information about storage classes, see Storage Classes in the *Amazon Simple Storage Service Developer Guide*.

      To change the storage class after you upload an object, choose **Storage class**. Choose the storage class that you want, and then choose **Save**.

   2. **Encryption** – You can encrypt your S3 objects. For more information, see How Do I Add Encryption to an S3 Object?.

   3. **Metadata** – Each object in Amazon S3 has a set of name-value pairs that represents its metadata. For information on adding metadata to an S3 object, see How Do I Add Metadata to an S3 Object?.

   4. **Tags** – You can add tags to an S3 object. For more information, see How Do I Add Tags to an S3 Object?.

How Do I Add Encryption to an S3 Object?

This topic describes how to set or change the type of encryption an object is using.

To add encryption to an object

1. Sign in to the AWS Management Console and open the Amazon S3 console at https://console.aws.amazon.com/s3/.

2. In the **Bucket name** list, choose the name of the bucket that contains the object.

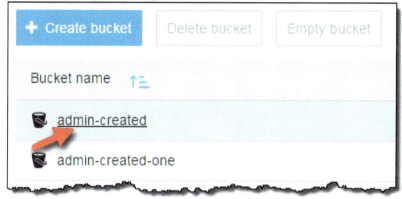

3. In the **Name** list, choose the name of the object that you want to add encryption to.

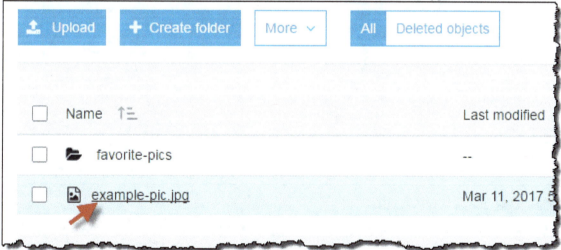

4. Choose **Properties**, and then choose **Encryption**.

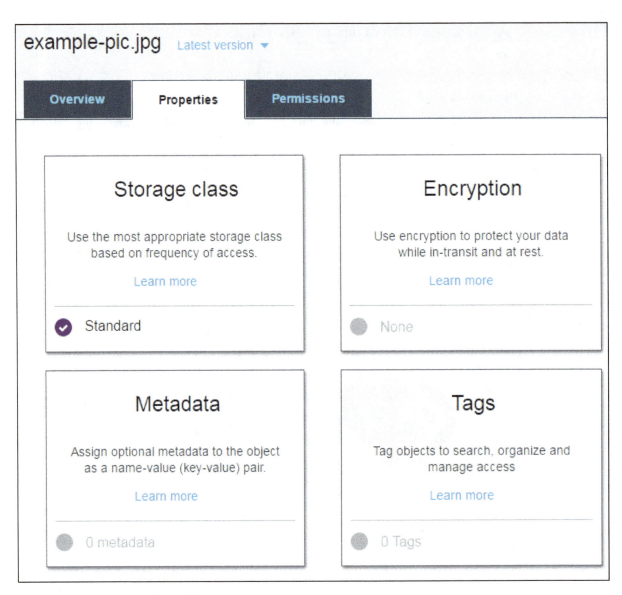

example-pic.jpg   Latest version ▼

| Overview | Properties | Permissions |

Storage class

Use the most appropriate storage class based on frequency of access.

Learn more

✓ Standard

Encryption

Use encryption to protect your data while in-transit and at rest.

Learn more

● None

Metadata

Assign optional metadata to the object as a name-value (key-value) pair.

Learn more

● 0 metadata

Tags

Tag objects to search, organize and manage access

Learn more

● 0 Tags

5. Select **AES-256** or **AWS-KMS**.

   1. To encrypt your object using keys that are managed by Amazon S3, select **AES-256**. For more information about using Amazon S3 server-side encryption to encrypt your data, see Protecting Data with Amazon S3-Managed Encryption Keys Classes in the *Amazon Simple Storage Service Developer Guide*.

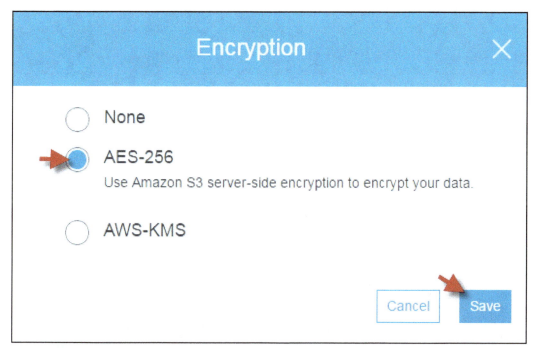

2. To encrypt your object using AWS Key Management Service (AWS KMS), choose **AWS-KMS**, choose a master key from the list of the AWS KMS master keys that you have created, and then choose **Save. Note**
To encrypt objects in the bucket, you can use only keys that are enabled in the same AWS Region as the bucket.

For more information about creating an AWS KMS key, see Creating Keys in the *AWS Key Management Service Developer Guide.* For more information, see Protecting Data with AWS KMS–Managed Key in the *Amazon Simple Storage Service Developer Guide.*

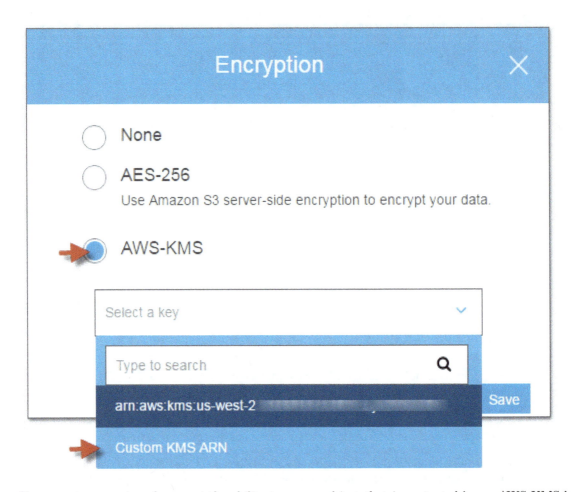

You can give an external account the ability to use an object that is protected by an AWS KMS key. To do this, select **Custom KMS ARN** from the list, type the Amazon Resource Name (ARN) for the external account, and then choose **Save**. Administrators of an external account that have usage permissions to an object protected by your AWS KMS key can further restrict access by creating a resource-level AWS Identity and Access Management (IAM) policy.

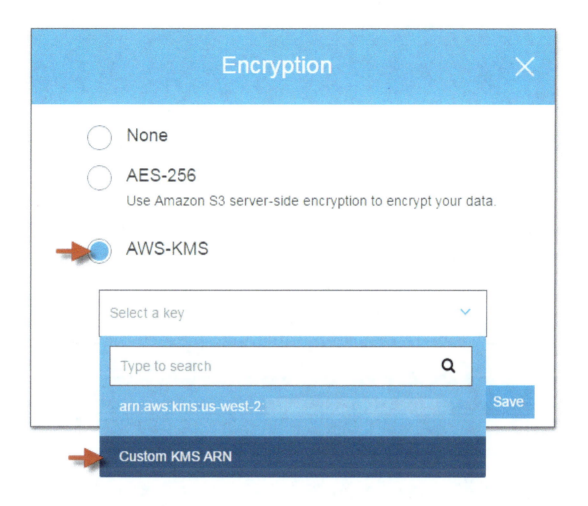

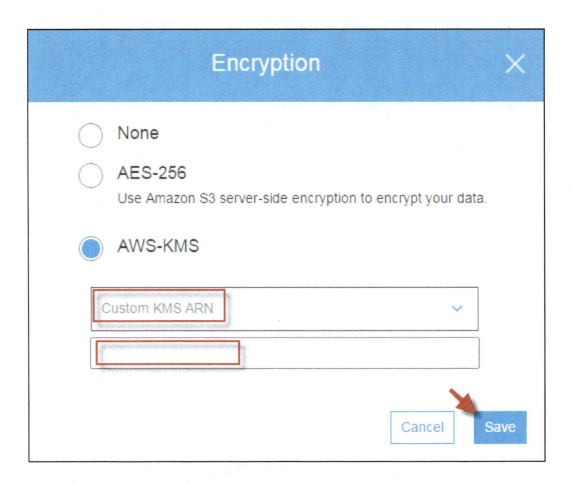

More Info

- How Do I View the Properties of an Object?
- Uploading, Downloading, and Managing Objects

How Do I Add Metadata to an S3 Object?

Each object in Amazon Simple Storage Service (Amazon S3) has a set of name-value pairs that provides metadata about the object. *Metadata* is additional information about the object. Some metadata is set by Amazon S3 when you upload the object, for example,`Date` and `Content-Length`. You can also set some metadata when you upload the object, or you can add it later. This section explains how to use the Amazon S3 console to add metadata to an S3 object.

Object metadata is a set of name-value (key-value) pairs. For example, the metadata for content length, `Content-Length`, is the name (key) and the size of the object in bytes (value). For more information about object metadata, see Object Metadata in the *Amazon Simple Storage Service Developer Guide*.

There are two kinds of metadata for an S3 object, Amazon S3 system metadata and user-defined metadata:

- **System metadata**–There are two categories of system metadata. Metadata such as the `Last-Modified` date is controlled by the system. Only Amazon S3 can modify the value. There is also system metadata that you control, for example, the storage class configured for the object.

- **User-defined metadata**–You can define your own custom metadata, called user-defined metadata. You can assign user-defined metadata to an object when you upload the object or after the object has been uploaded. User-defined metadata is stored with the object and is returned when you download the object. Amazon S3 does not process user-defined metadata.

The following topics describe how to add metadata to an object.

Adding System-Defined Metadata to an S3 Object

You can configure some system metadata for an S3 object. For a list of system-defined metadata and whether you can modify their values, see System-Defined Metadata in the *Amazon Simple Storage Service Developer Guide*.

To add system metadata to an object

1. Sign in to the AWS Management Console and open the Amazon S3 console at https://console.aws.amazon.com/s3/.

2. In the **Bucket name** list, choose the name of the bucket that contains the object.

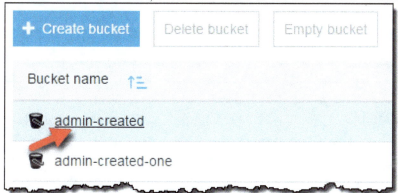

3. In the **Name** list, choose the name of the object that you want to add metadata to.

4. Choose **Properties**, and then choose **Metadata**.

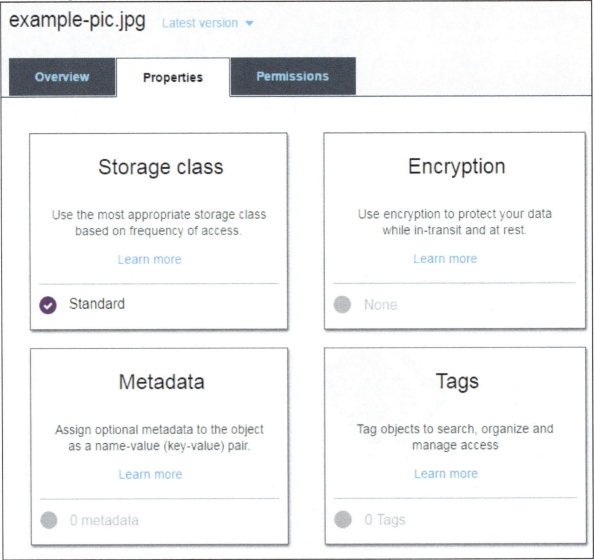

5. Choose **Add Metadata**, and then choose a key from the **Select a key** menu.

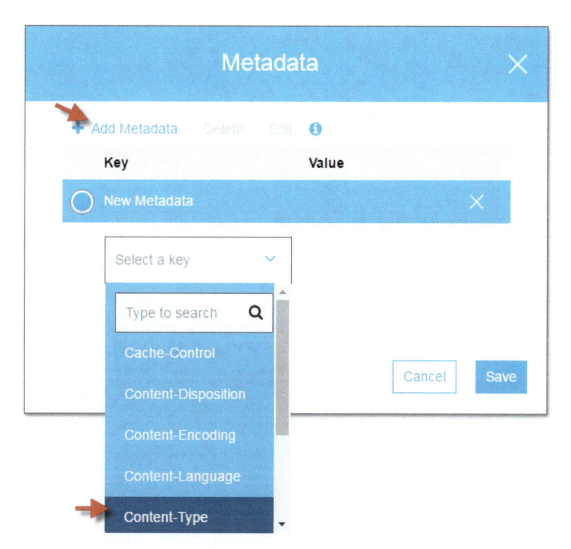

6. Depending on which key you chose, choose a value from the **Select a value** menu or type a value.

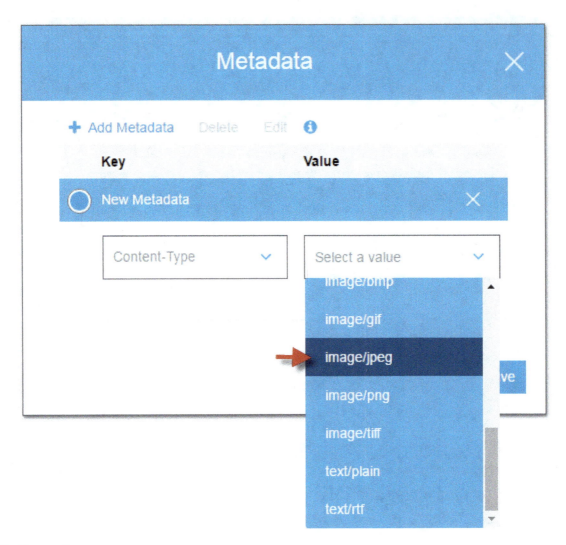

7. Choose **Save**.

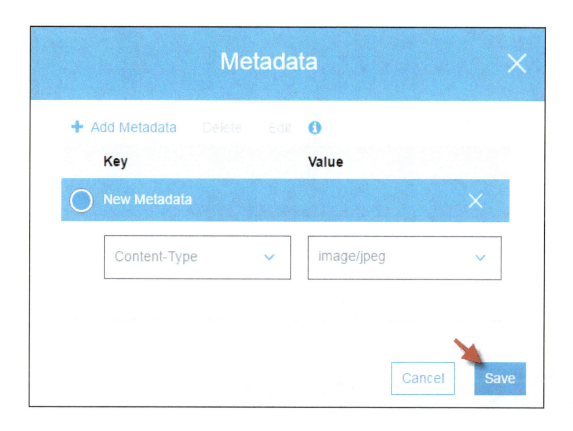

Adding User-Defined Metadata to an S3 Object

You can assign user-defined metadata to an object. User-defined metadata must begin with the prefix "x-amz-meta-", otherwise Amazon S3 will not set the key value pair as you define it. You define custom metadata by adding a name that you choose to the x-amz-meta- key. This creates a custom key. For example, if you add the custom name alt-name, the metadata key would be x-amz-meta-alt-name.

User-defined metadata can be as large as 2 KB. Both keys and their values must conform to US-ASCII standards. For more information, see User-Defined Metadata in the *Amazon Simple Storage Service Developer Guide*.

To add user-defined metadata to an object

1. Sign in to the AWS Management Console and open the Amazon S3 console at https://console.aws.amazon.com/s3/.

2. In the **Bucket name** list, choose the name of the bucket that contains the object.

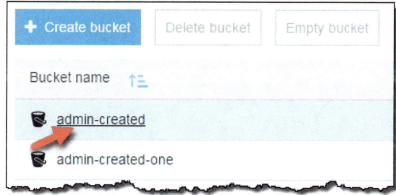

3. In the **Name** list, choose the name of the object that you want to add metadata to.

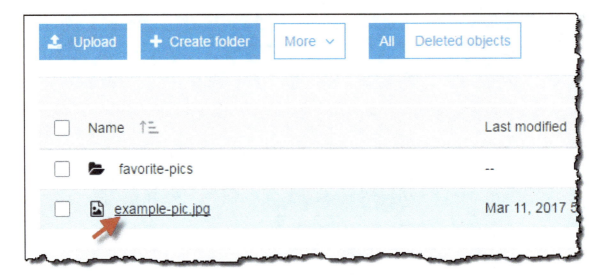

4. Choose **Properties**, and then choose **Metadata**.

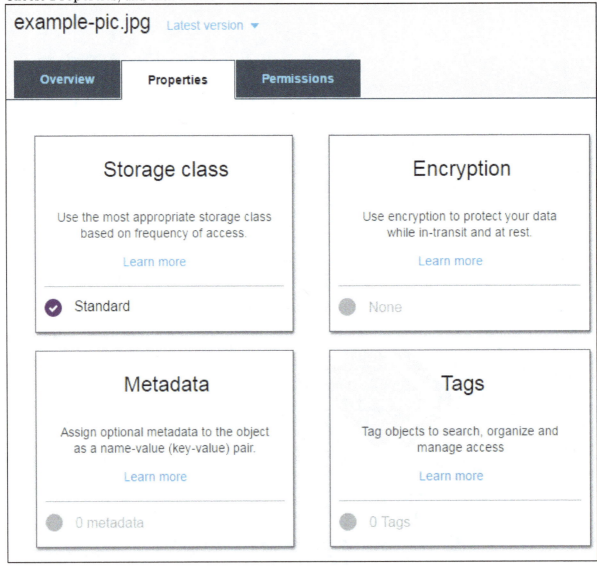

5. Choose **Add Metadata**, and then choose the `x-amz-meta-` key from the **Select a key** menu. Any

metadata starting with the prefix `x-amz-meta-` is user-defined metadata.

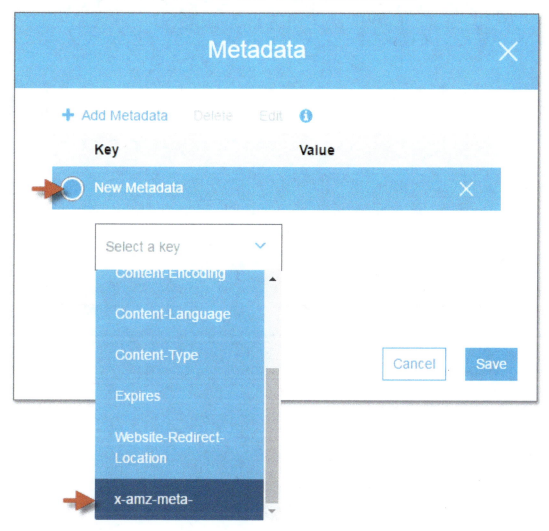

6. Type a custom name following the `x-amz-meta-` key. For example, for the custom name `alt-name`, the metadata key would be `x-amz-meta-alt-name`. Enter a value for the custom key, and then choose **Save**.

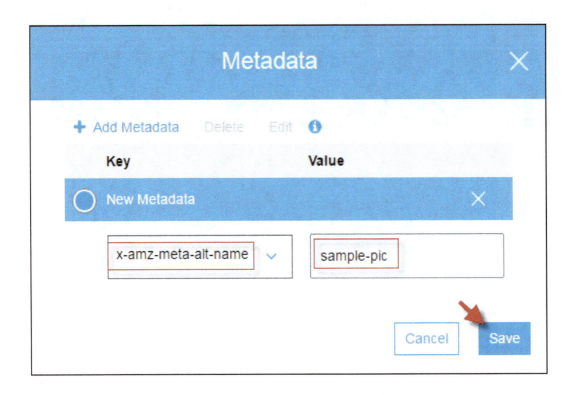

- How Do I View the Properties of an Object?
- Uploading, Downloading, and Managing Objects

How Do I Add Tags to an S3 Object?

This topic explains how to use the console to add tags to an S3 object. For information about object tags, see Object Tagging in the *Amazon Simple Storage Service Developer Guide*

To add tags to an object

1. Sign in to the AWS Management Console and open the Amazon S3 console at https://console.aws.amazon.com/s3/.

2. In the **Bucket name** list, choose the name of the bucket that contains the object.

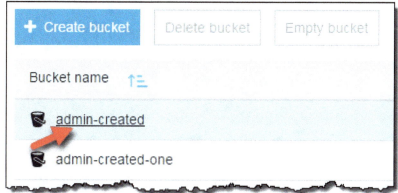

3. In the **Name** list, choose the name of the object you want to add tags to.

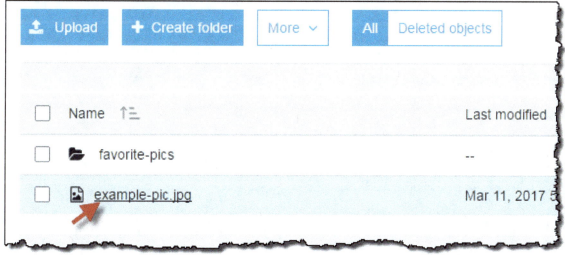

4. Choose **Properties**.

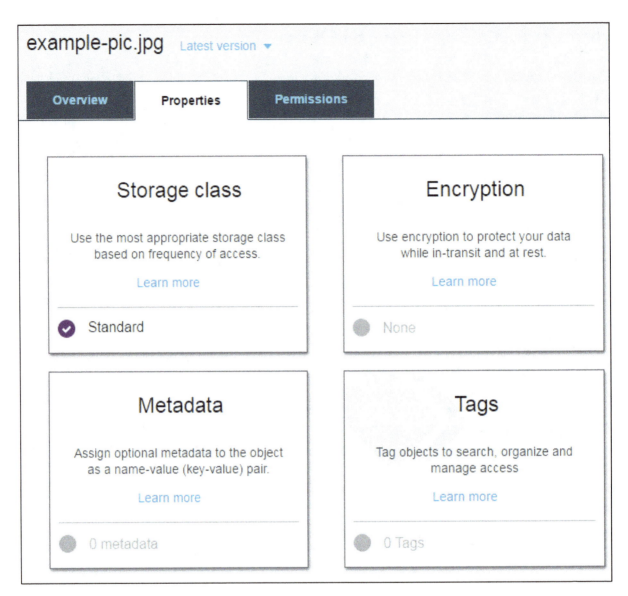

5. Choose **Tags** and then choose **Add Tag**.

6. Choose **Tags** and then choose **Add Tag**.

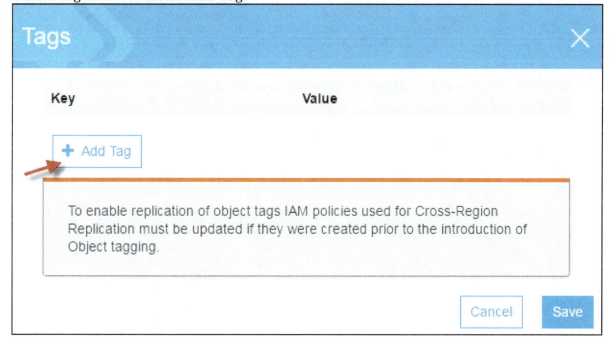

7. Each tag is a key-value pair. Type a **Key** and a **Value**. Then choose **Add Tag** to add another tag or choose **Save**.

   You can enter up to 10 tags for an object.

More Info

- How Do I View the Properties of an Object?
- Uploading, Downloading, and Managing Objects

Storage Management

This section explains how to configure Amazon S3 storage management tools.

How Do I Create a Lifecycle Policy for an S3 Bucket?

You can use lifecycle policies to define actions you want Amazon S3 to take during an object's lifetime (for example, transition objects to another storage class, archive them, or delete them after a specified period of time).

You can define a lifecycle policy for all objects or a subset of objects in the bucket by using a shared prefix (that is, objects that have names that begin with a common string).

A versioning-enabled bucket can have many versions of the same object, one current version and zero or more noncurrent (previous) versions. Using a lifecycle policy, you can define actions specific to current and noncurrent object versions. For more information, see Object Lifecycle Management and Object Versioning and Using Versioning in the *Amazon Simple Storage Service Developer Guide*.

To create a lifecycle policy

1. Sign in to the AWS Management Console and open the Amazon S3 console at https://console.aws.amazon.com/s3/.

2. In the **Bucket name** list, choose the name of the bucket that you want to create a lifecycle policy for.

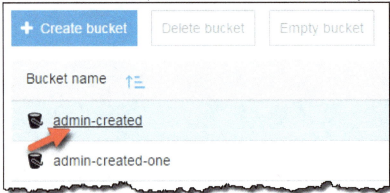

3. Choose the **Management** tab, and then choose **Add lifecycle rule**.

1. If the bucket does not have a lifecycle policy, you can choose **Get started**.

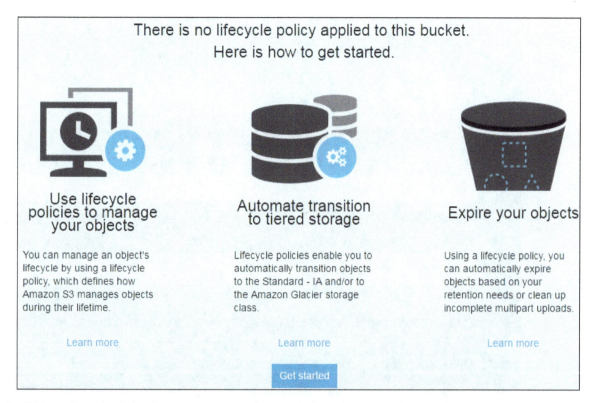

There is no lifecycle policy applied to this bucket.
Here is how to get started.

Use lifecycle policies to manage your objects

You can manage an object's lifecycle by using a lifecycle policy, which defines how Amazon S3 manages objects during their lifetime.

Learn more

Automate transition to tiered storage

Lifecycle policies enable you to automatically transition objects to the Standard - IA and/or to the Amazon Glacier storage class.

Learn more

Expire your objects

Using a lifecycle policy, you can automatically expire objects based on your retention needs or clean up incomplete multipart uploads.

Learn more

Get started

4. In the **Lifecycle rule** dialog box, type a name for your rule to help identify the rule later. The name must be unique within the bucket. Configure the rule as follows:

- To apply this lifecycle rule to all objects with a specified name prefix (that is, objects with names that begin with a common string), type in a prefix. You can also limit the lifecycle rule scope to one or more object tags. You can combine a prefix and tags. For more information about object name prefixes, see Object Keys in the *Amazon Simple Storage Service Developer Guide*. For more information about object tags, see Object Tagging in the *Amazon Simple Storage Service Developer Guide*

- To apply this lifecycle rule to all objects in the bucket, choose **Next**.

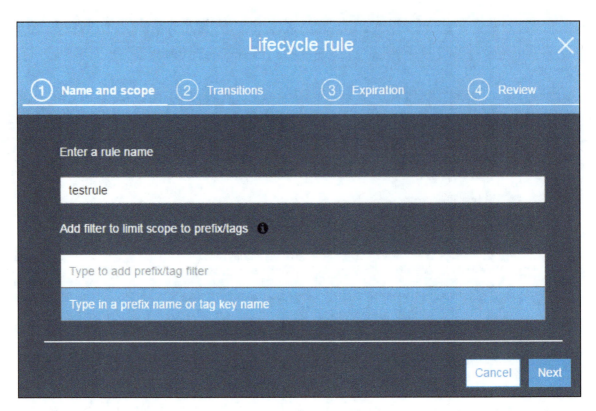

5. You configure lifecycle rules by defining rules to transition objects to the Standard-IA and Amazon Glacier storage classes. For more information, see Storage Classes in the *Amazon Simple Storage Service Developer Guide*.

You can define transitions for current or previous object versions, or for both current and previous versions. Versioning enables you to keep multiple versions of an object in one bucket. For more information about versioning, see How Do I Enable or Suspend Versioning for an S3 Bucket?.

1. Select **Current version** to define transitions that are applied to the current version of the object.

   Select **Previous version** to define transitions that are applied to all previous versions of the object.

   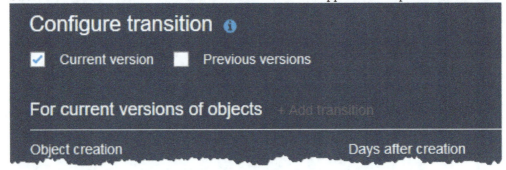

2. Choose **Add transitions** and specify one of the following transitions:

   - Choose **Transition to Standard-IA after**, and then type the number of days after the creation of an object that you want the transition to be applied (for example, 30 days).

   - Choose **Transition to Amazon Glacier after**, and then type the number of days after the creation of an object that you want the transition to be applied (for example, 100 days).

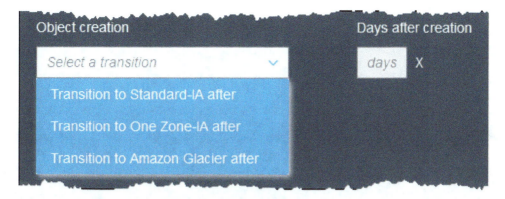

6. When you are done configuring transitions, choose **Next**.

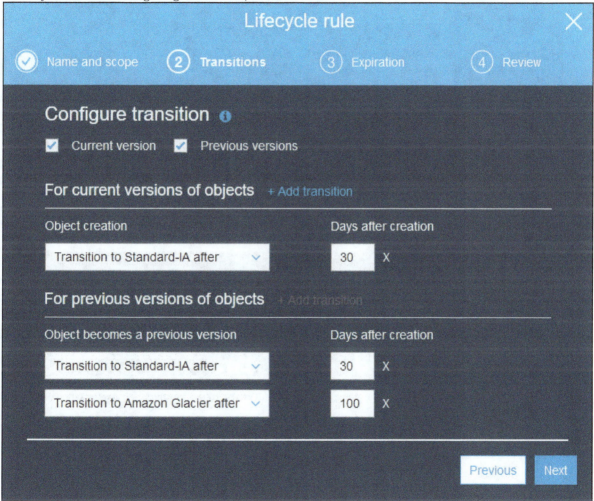

7. Select **Expiration** and then enter the number of days after object creation to delete the object (for example, 455 days).

8. Select **Permanently delete previous versions** and then enter the number of days after an object becomes a previous version to permanently delete the object (for example, 455 days).

9. It is a recommended best practice to always select **Clean up incomplete multipart uploads**. For example, type 7 for the number of days after the multipart upload initiation date that you want to end and clean up any multipart uploads that have not completed. For more information about multipart uploads, see Multipart Upload Overview in the Amazon Simple Storage Service Developer Guide.

10. Choose **Next**.

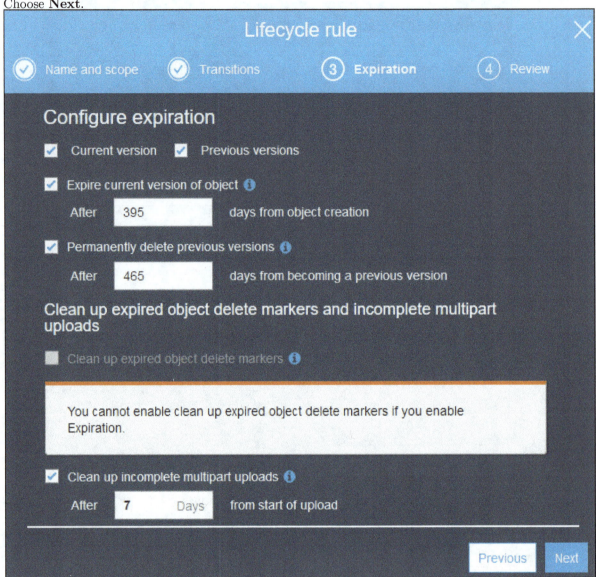

11. For **Review**, verify the settings for your rule. If you need to make changes, choose **Previous**. Otherwise, choose **Save**.

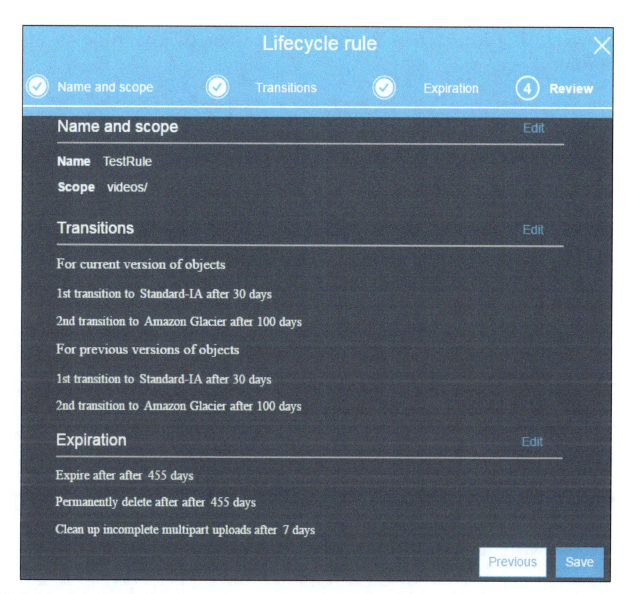

Lifecycle rule

✓ Name and scope   ✓ Transitions   ✓ Expiration   ④ **Review**

Name and scope   Edit

Name   TestRule

Scope   videos/

Transitions   Edit

For current version of objects

1st transition to Standard-IA after 30 days

2nd transition to Amazon Glacier after 100 days

For previous versions of objects

1st transition to Standard-IA after 30 days

2nd transition to Amazon Glacier after 100 days

Expiration   Edit

Expire after after 455 days

Permanently delete after after 455 days

Clean up incomplete multipart uploads after 7 days

Previous   Save

12. If the rule does not contain any errors, it is listed on the **Lifecycle** page and is enabled.

+ Add lifecycle rule   Edit   Delete   More ⌄

	Lifecycle rule	Applied to	Actions for current version	Actions for previous version(s)
✓	testrule	Whole bucket	Standard-IA / Expire	Standard-IA / Amazon Glacier / Permanently Delete

How Do I Add a Cross-Region Replication (CRR) Rule to an S3 Bucket?

Cross-region replication is the automatic, asynchronous copying of objects across buckets in different AWS Regions. Cross-region replication replicates newly created objects, object updates, and object deletions from a source bucket to a destination bucket in a different AWS Region.

Cross-region replication requires that the source and destination buckets be in different AWS Regions, and versioning must be enabled on both the source and destination buckets. To review the full list of requirements, see Requirements for Cross-Region Replication in the *Amazon Simple Storage Service Developer Guide*. For more information about versioning, see How Do I Enable or Suspend Versioning for an S3 Bucket?.

The object replicas in the destination bucket are exact replicas of the objects in the source bucket. They have the same key names and the same metadata—for example, creation time, owner, user-defined metadata, version ID, access control list (ACL), and storage class. Optionally, you can explicitly specify a different storage class for object replicas. And regardless of who owns the source bucket or the source object, you can choose to change replica ownership to the AWS account that owns the destination bucket. For more information, see CRR: Change Replica Owner in the *Amazon Simple Storage Service Developer Guide*.

The time it takes for Amazon S3 to replicate an object depends on the object size. It can take up to several hours to replicate a large-sized object.

Note about replication and lifecycle rules

Metadata for an object remains identical between original objects and replica objects. Lifecycle rules abide by the creation time of the original object, and not by when the replicated object becomes available in the destination bucket. However, lifecycle does not act on objects that are pending replication until replication is complete.

You use the Amazon S3 console to add replication rules to the source bucket. Replication rules define which source bucket objects to replicate and the destination bucket where the replicated objects are stored. You can create rules to replicate all the objects in a bucket or a subset of objects with specific key name prefixes (that is, objects that have names that begin with a common string). A destination bucket can be in the same AWS account as the source bucket, or it can be in a different account. The destination bucket must always be in a different Region than the source bucket.

If the destination bucket is in a different account from the source bucket, you must add a bucket policy to the destination bucket to grant the owner of the source bucket account permission to replicate objects in the destination bucket. The Amazon S3 console builds this required bucket policy for you to copy and add to the destination bucket in the other account.

When you add a replication rule to a bucket, the rule is enabled by default, so it starts working as soon as you save it.

Adding a Cross-Region Replication Rule to an S3 Bucket

To add a cross-region replication rule to an S3 bucket

1. Sign in to the AWS Management Console and open the Amazon S3 console at https://console.aws.amazon.com/s3/.

2. In the **Bucket name** list, choose the name of the bucket that you want.

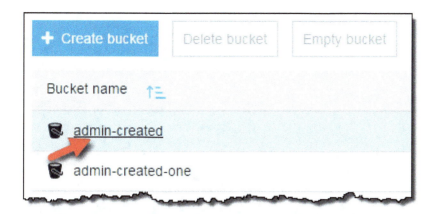

3. Choose **Management**, choose **Replication**, and then choose **Add rule**.

4. To replicate the whole bucket, in the **Replication rule** dialog box, under **Source**, choose **All contents in** *bucket-name*. To replicate all objects that have the same prefix (for example, all objects that have names that begin with the string `pictures`), choose **Prefix in this bucket**. For example, all objects in a folder named pictures. If you enter a prefix that is the name of a folder, you must use / (forward slash) as the last character (for example, `pictures/`).

Under **Status**, **Enabled** is selected by default. An enabled rule starts to work as soon as you save it. If you want to enable the rule later, select **Disabled**.

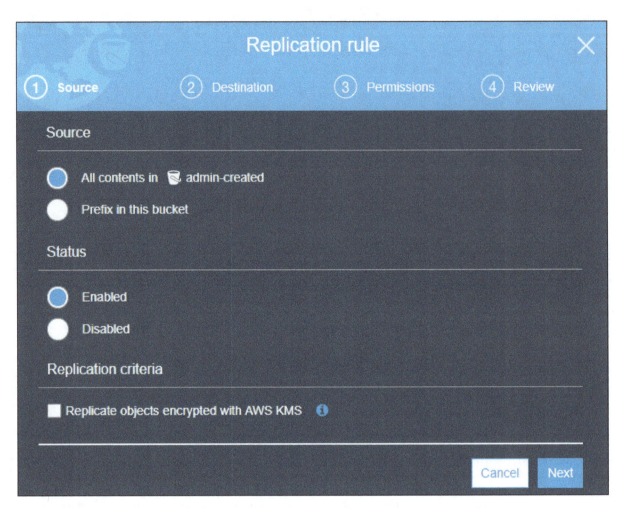

5. To replicate objects in the source bucket that are encrypted with AWS KMS, under **Replication criteria**, select **Replicate objects encrypted with AWS KMS**. Under **Choose one or more keys for decrypting source objects** are the source AWS KMS key or keys that you allow cross-region replication to use. All source keys are included by default. You can choose to narrow the key selection.

Objects encrypted by AWS KMS keys that you do not select are not replicated by cross-region replication. A key or a group of keys is chosen for you, but you can choose the keys if you want. For information about using AWS KMS with cross-region replication, see CRR: Replicating Objects Created with Server-Side Encryption (SSE) Using AWS KMS-Managed Encryption Key in the *Amazon Simple Storage Service Developer Guide*.

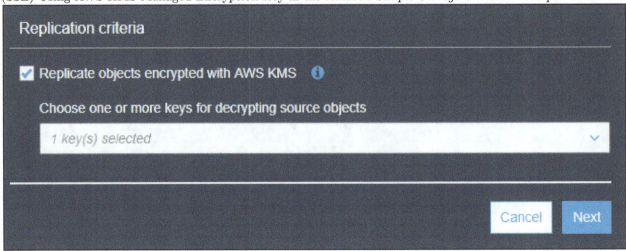

Important

AWS KMS has a request rate limit. For more information, see AWS KMS limits. AWS KMS support for cross-region replication increases the KMS request rate for your account. As a best practice, we recommend requesting an increase in your AWS KMS API rate limit by creating a case in the AWS Support Center. For information about contacting AWS Support, see Contact Us. We recommend confirming the rate limit increase before enabling cross-region replication with AWS KMS.

Choose **Next**.

1. To choose a destination bucket from the account that you're currently using, on the **Destination** page, under **Destination bucket**, choose **Buckets in this account**. Type the name of the destination bucket for the replication, or choose a name in the drop-down list. If you don't see the bucket that you want in the list, confirm that the bucket exists and that it's in a different Region than the source bucket.

   If you want to choose a destination bucket from a different AWS account, see Configuring a CRR Rule When the Destination Bucket is in a Different AWS Account.

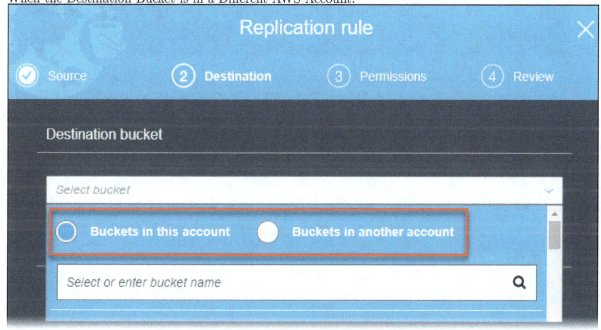

   If versioning is not enabled on the destination bucket, you get a warning message that contains an **Enable versioning** button. Choose this button to enable versioning on the bucket.

111

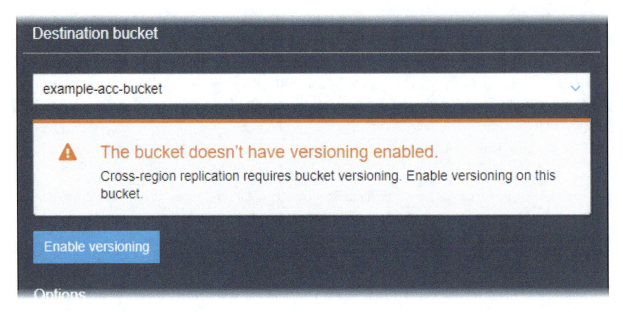

2. If you chose to replicate objects encrypted with AWS KMS, under **Destination encryption settings**, type the Amazon Resource Name (ARN) of the AWS KMS key to use to encrypt the replicas in the destination bucket. You can find the ARN for your AWS KMS key in the IAM console, under **Encryption keys**. Or, you can choose a key name from the drop-down list.

For more information about creating an AWS KMS key, see Creating Keys in the *AWS Key Management Service Developer Guide*.

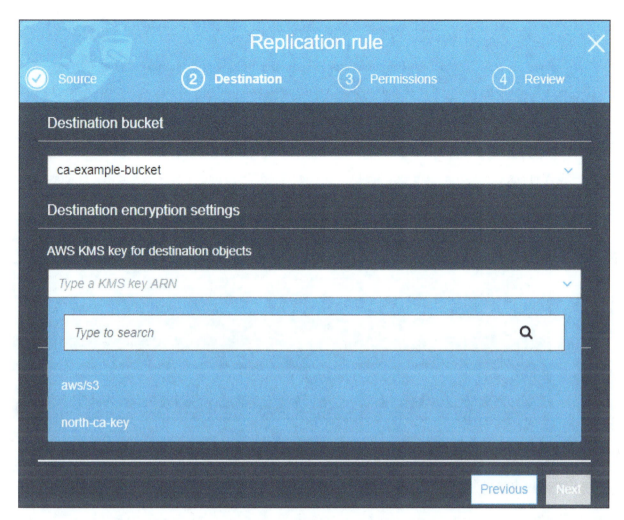

3. If you want to replicate your data into a specific storage class in the destination bucket, on the **Destination** page, under **Options**, select **Change the storage class for the replicated object(s)**. Then choose the storage class that you want to use for the replicated objects in the destination bucket. If you don't select this option, the storage class for replicated objects is the same class as the original objects.

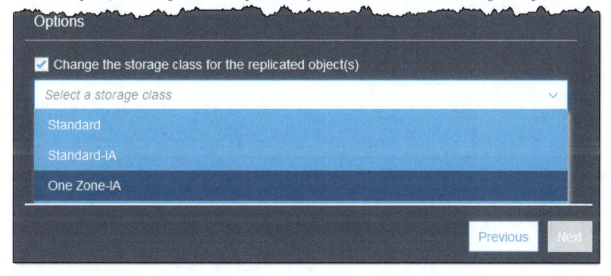

Choose **Next**.

4. Set up an AWS Identity and Access Management (IAM) role that Amazon S3 can assume to perform cross-region replication of objects on your behalf.

To set up an IAM role, on the **Permissions** page, under **Select role**, do one of the following:

- We highly recommend that you choose **Create new role** to have Amazon S3 create a new IAM role for you. When you save the rule, a new policy is generated for the IAM role that matches the source and destination buckets that you choose. The name of the generated role is based on the bucket names and uses the following naming convention: **replication_role_for_*source-bucket*_to_*destination-bucket***.

- You can choose to use an existing IAM role. If you do, you must choose a role that grants Amazon S3 the necessary permissions for replication. Replication fails if this role does not grant Amazon S3 sufficient permissions to follow your replication rule.

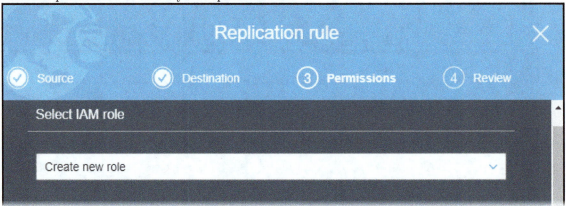

Choose **Next**.

5. On the **Review** page, review your replication rule. If it looks correct, choose **Save**. Otherwise, choose **Previous** to edit the rule before saving it.

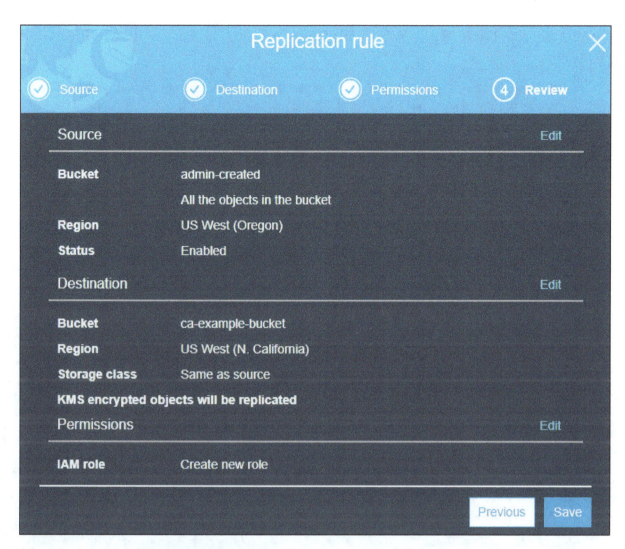

6. After you save your rule, you can edit, enable, disable, or delete your rule on the **Replication** page.

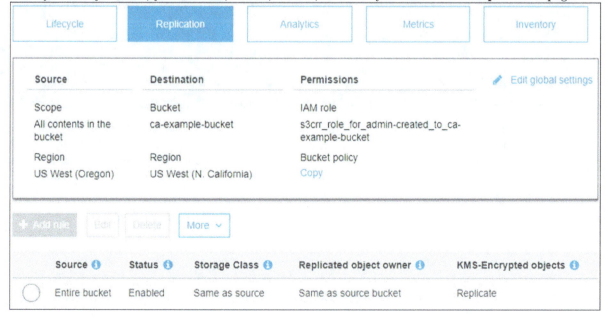

Configuring a CRR Rule When the Destination Bucket is in a Different AWS Account

This section describes how to configure cross-region replication rule when the destination bucket is in a different AWS account than the source bucket.

To add a cross-region replication rule when the destination bucket is in a different AWS account than the source bucket

1. If you have never created a cross-region replication rule before, start with Adding a Cross-Region Replication Rule to an S3 Bucket.

   On the **Replication rule** wizard **Destination** page, under **Destination bucket**, choose **Buckets in another account**. Then type the name of the destination bucket and the account ID from a different AWS account. Choose **Save**.

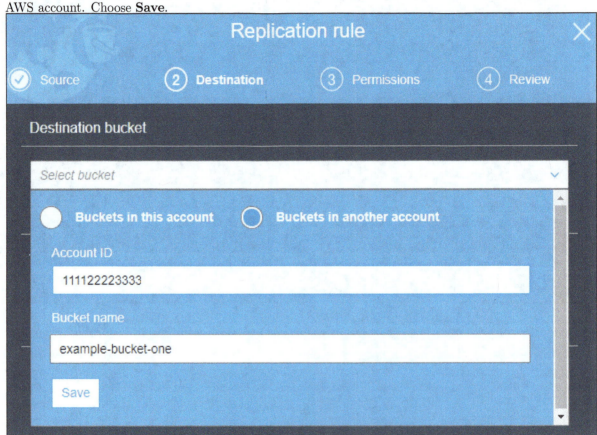

After you save the destination bucket name and account ID, you might get a warning message indicating that you must add a bucket policy to the destination bucket so that Amazon S3 can verify whether versioning is enabled on the bucket. You can copy the bucket policy from the **Permissions** page, and then add the policy to the destination bucket in the other account. For information about adding a bucket policy to an S3 bucket, see How Do I Add an S3 Bucket Policy?.

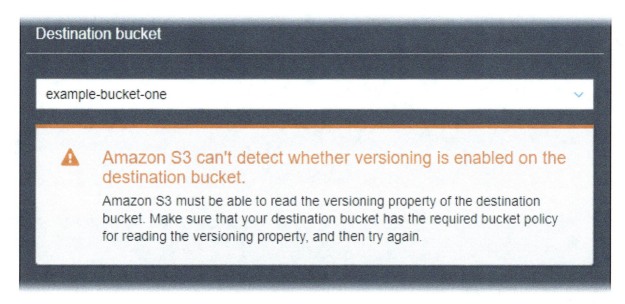

2. If you chose to replicate objects encrypted with AWS KMS, under **Destination encryption settings**, type the Amazon Resource Name (ARN) AWS KMS key to use to encrypt the replicas in the destination bucket.

   For more information about creating an AWS KMS key, see Creating Keys in the *AWS Key Management Service Developer Guide*.

3. If you want to replicate your data into a specific storage class in the destination bucket, on the **Destination** page, under **Options**, select **Change the storage class for the replicated object(s)**. Then choose the storage class that you want to use for the replicated objects in the destination bucket. If you don't select this option, the storage class for replicated objects is the same class as the original objects.

4. To change the object ownership of the replica objects to the destination bucket owner, under **Options**, select **Change object ownership to destination owner**. This option enables you to separate object ownership of the replicated data from the source. If asked, type the account ID of the destination bucket.

   When you select this option, regardless of who owns the source bucket or the source object, the AWS account that owns the destination bucket is granted full permission to replica objects. For more information, see CRR: Change Replica Owner in the *Amazon Simple Storage Service Developer Guide*.

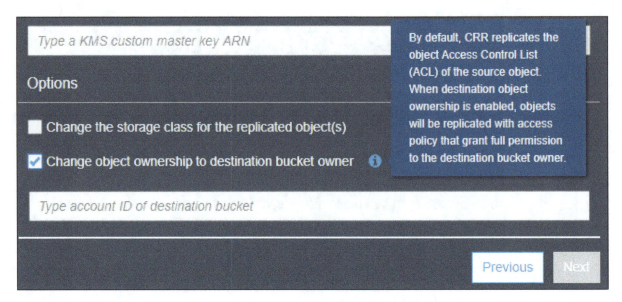

5. Set up an AWS Identity and Access Management (IAM) role that Amazon S3 can assume to perform cross-region replication of objects on your behalf.

   To set up an IAM role, on the **Permissions** page, under **Select role**, do one of the following:

   - We highly recommend that you choose **Create new role** to have Amazon S3 create a new IAM role for you. When you save the rule, a new policy is generated for the IAM role that matches the source and destination buckets that you choose. The name of the generated role is based on the bucket names and uses the following naming convention: **replication_role_for_*source-bucket*_to_*destination-bucket***.

   - You can choose to use an existing IAM role. If you do, you must choose a role that allows Amazon S3 to replicate objects from the source bucket to the destination bucket on your behalf.

6. A bucket policy is provided on the **Permissions** page that you can copy and add to the destination bucket in the other account. For information about adding a bucket policy to an S3 bucket, see How Do I Add an S3 Bucket Policy?.

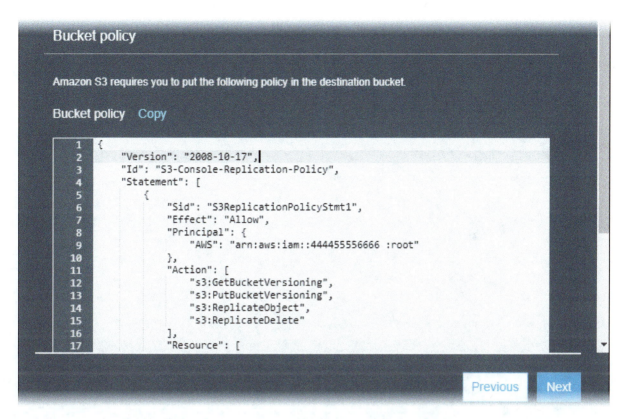

7. If you chose to replicate objects encrypted with AWS KMS, an AWS KMS key policy is provided on the **Permissions** page. You can copy this policy to add to the key policy for the AWS KMS key customer master key (CMK) that you are using. The key policy grants the source bucket owner permission to use the key. For information about updating the key policy, see Grant the Source Bucket Owner Permission to Encrypt Using the AWS KMS Key.

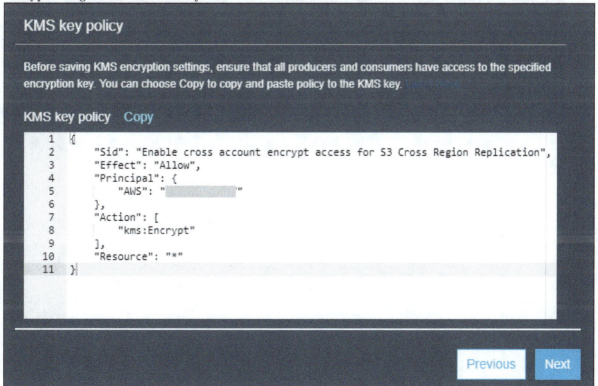

8. On the **Review** page, review your replication rule. If it looks correct, choose **Save**. Otherwise, choose **Previous** to edit the rule before saving it.

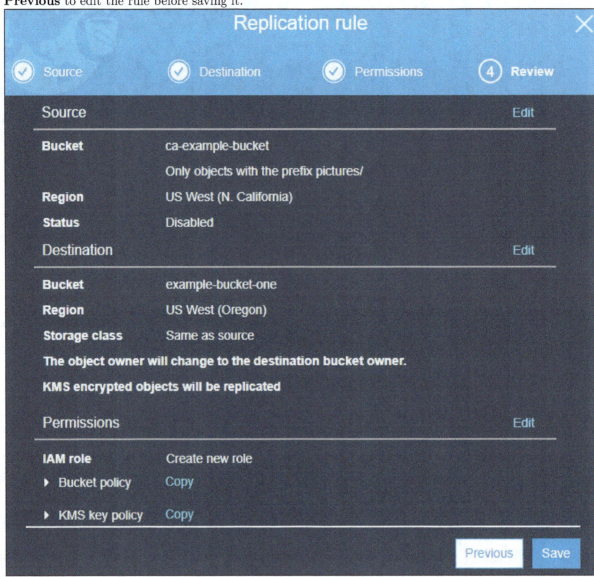

9. After you save your rule, you can edit, enable, disable, or delete your rule on the **Replication** page.

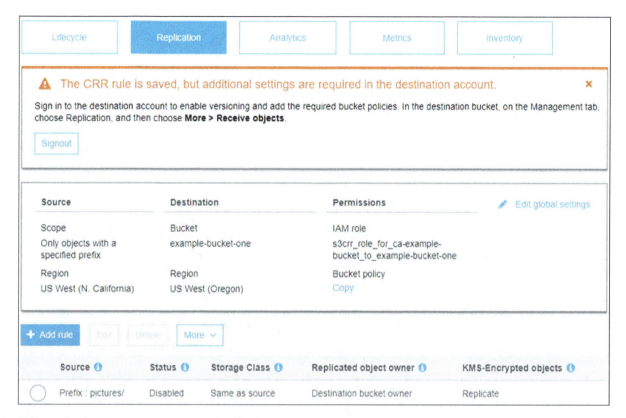

10. Follow the instructions given on the Replication page under the warning message **The CRR rule is saved, but additional settings are required in the destination account.** Sign out of the AWS account that you are currently in, and then sign in to the destination account. **Important** Cross-region replication fails until you sign in to the destination account and complete the following steps.

11. After you sign in to the destination account, choose the **Management** tab, choose Replication, and then choose **Receive objects** from the **More **menu.

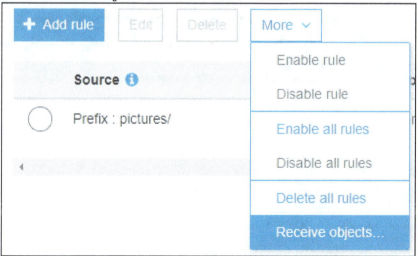

12. From the Receive objects page, you can perform the following:

- Enable versioning on the destination bucket.

- Apply the bucket policy provided by Amazon S3 to the destination bucket.

- Copy the AWS KMS key policy that you need to update the AWS KMS CMK key that is being used to encrypt the replica objects in the destination bucket. For information about updating the key policy, see Grant the Source Bucket Owner Permission to Encrypt Using the AWS KMS Key.

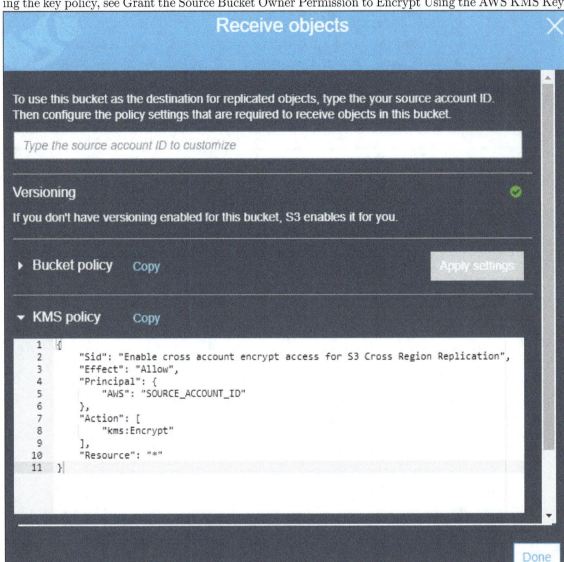

Grant the Source Bucket Owner Permission to Encrypt Using the AWS KMS Key

You must grant permissions to the account of the source bucket owner to encrypt using your AWS KMS key with a key policy. The following procedure describes how to use the AWS Identity and Access Management (IAM) console to modify the key policy for the AWS KMS customer master key (CMK) that is being used to encrypt the replica objects in the destination bucket.

To grant permissions to encrypt using your AWS KMS key

1. Sign in to the AWS Management Console using the AWS account that owns the AWS KMS CMK. Open the IAM console at https://console.aws.amazon.com/iam/.

2. In the left navigation pane, choose **Encryption keys**.

3. For **Region**, choose the appropriate AWS Region. Do not use the region selector in the navigation bar (upper-right corner).

4. Choose the alias of the CMK that you want to encrypt with.

5. In the **Key Policy** section of the page, choose **Switch to policy view**.

6. Using the **Key Policy** editor, insert the key policy provided by Amazon S3 into the existing key policy, and then choose **Save Changes**. You might want to add the policy to the end of the existing policy.

For more information about creating and editing AWS KMS CMKs, see Getting Started in the *AWS Key Management Service Developer Guide.*

More Info

- How Do I Manage the Cross-Region Replication Rules for an S3 Bucket?
- How Do I Enable or Suspend Versioning for an S3 Bucket?
- Cross-Region Replication in the *Amazon Simple Storage Service Developer Guide*

How Do I Manage the Cross-Region Replication Rules for an S3 Bucket?

Cross-region replication is the automatic, asynchronous copying of objects across buckets in different AWS Regions. It replicates newly created objects, object updates, and object deletions from a source bucket to a destination bucket in a different Region.

You use the Amazon S3 console to add replication rules to the source bucket. Replication rules define the source bucket objects to replicate and the destination bucket where the replicated objects are stored. For more information about cross-region replication, see Cross-Region Replication in the *Amazon Simple Storage Service Developer Guide*.

You can manage replication rules on the **Replication** page. You can add, view, enable, disable, and delete the replication rules. For information about adding replication rules to a bucket, see How Do I Add a Cross-Region Replication (CRR) Rule to an S3 Bucket?.

To manage the cross-region replication rules for an S3 bucket

1. Sign in to the AWS Management Console and open the Amazon S3 console at https://console.aws.amazon.com/s3/.

2. In the **Bucket name** list, choose the name of the bucket that you want.

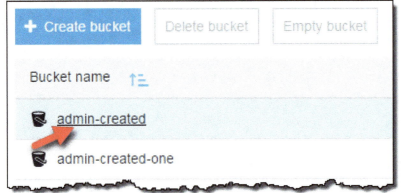

3. Choose **Management**, and then choose **Replication**.

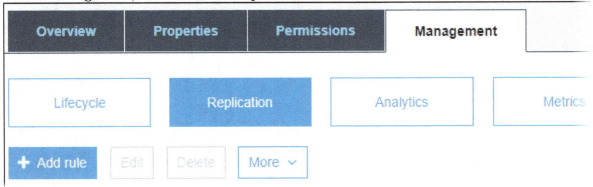

4. You change the replication rules in the following ways.

   - To change settings that affect all the replication rules in the bucket, choose **Edit global settings**.

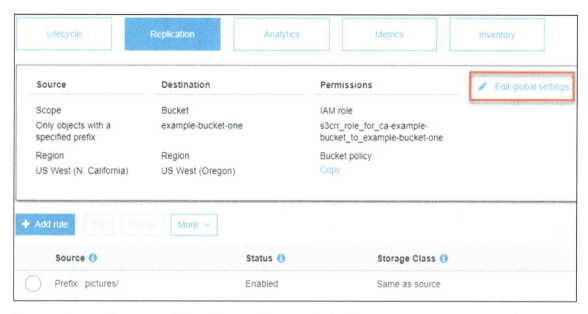

You can change the scope of the objects to be copied, the destination bucket, and the IAM role. If needed, you can copy the required bucket policy for cross-account destination buckets.

You can set the scope to **All contents** (for all objects in the bucket) or **Only objects with a specific prefix**. If the scope is **All contents**, there can be only one rule. When you choose a different scope, the Replication wizard starts to help you make the change. For information about using the wizard, see How Do I Add a Cross-Region Replication (CRR) Rule to an S3 Bucket?.

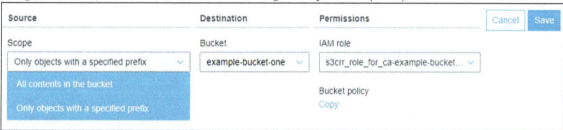

- To change a replication rule, select the rule and choose **Edit**, which starts the Replication wizard to help you make the change. For information about using the wizard, see How Do I Add a Cross-Region Replication (CRR) Rule to an S3 Bucket?.

- To enable or disable a replication rule, select the rule, choose **More**, and in the drop-down list, choose **Enable rule** or **Disable rule**. You can also disable, enable, or delete all the rules in the bucket from the **More** drop-down list.

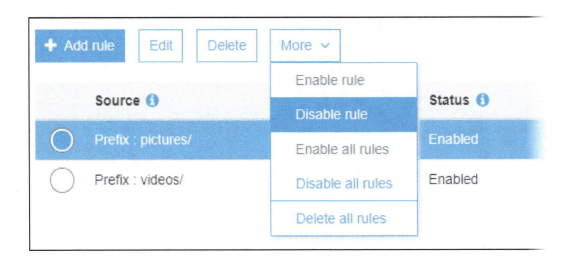

More Info

- How Do I Add a Cross-Region Replication (CRR) Rule to an S3 Bucket?
- Cross-Region Replication in the *Amazon Simple Storage Service Developer Guide*

How Do I Configure Storage Class Analysis?

By using the Amazon S3 analytics storage class analysis tool you can analyze storage access patterns to help you decide when to transition the right data to the right storage class. Storage class analysis observes data access patterns to help you determine when to transition less frequently accessed STANDARD storage to the STANDARD_IA (IA, for infrequent access) storage class. For more information about STANDARD_IA, see the Amazon S3 FAQ and Storage Classes in the *Amazon Simple Storage Service Developer Guide*.

For more information about analytics, see Amazon S3 Analytics – Storage Class Analysis in the *Amazon Simple Storage Service Developer Guide*.

To configure storage class analysis

1. Sign in to the AWS Management Console and open the Amazon S3 console at https://console.aws.amazon.com/s3/.

2. In the **Bucket name** list, choose the name of the bucket for which you want to configure storage class analysis.

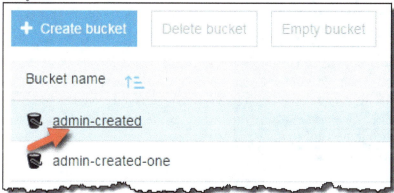

3. Choose the **Management** tab, and then choose **Analytics**.

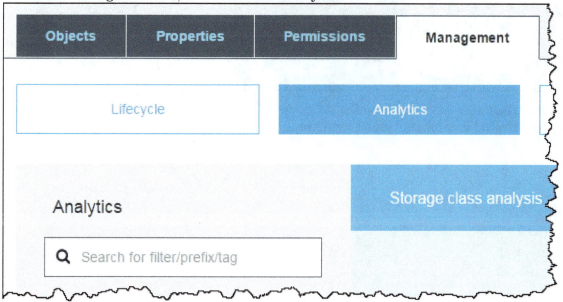

4. Choose **Add**.

5. Type a name for the filter. If you want to analyze the whole bucket, leave the **Prefix / tags **field empty.

6. In the **Prefix / tags ** field, type text for the prefix or tag for the objects that you want to analyze, or choose from the dropdown list that appears when you start typing.

7. If you chose **tag**, enter a value for the tag. You can enter one prefix and multiple tags.

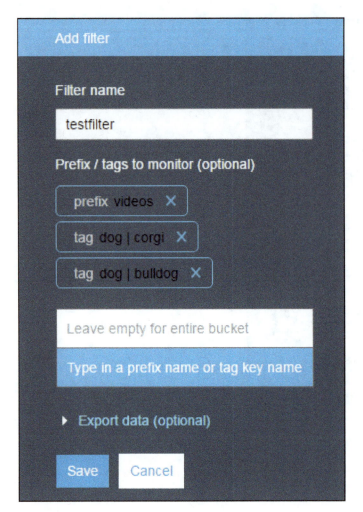

8. Optionally, you can choose **Export data** to export analysis reports to a comma-separated values (.csv) flat file. Choose a destination bucket where the file can be stored. You can type a prefix for the destination bucket. The destination bucket must be in the same AWS Region as the bucket for which you are setting up the analysis. The destination bucket can be in a different AWS account.

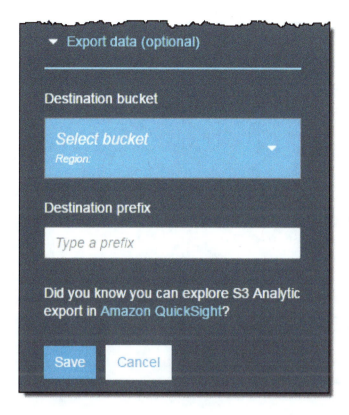

9. Choose **Save**.

Amazon S3 creates a bucket policy on the destination bucket that grants Amazon S3 write permission. This allow it to write the export data to the bucket.

If an error occurs when you try to create the bucket policy, you'll be given instructions on how to fix it. For example, if you chose a destination bucket in another AWS account and do not have permissions to read and write to the bucket policy, you'll see the following message. You must have the destination bucket owner add the displayed bucket policy to the destination bucket. If the policy is not added to the destination bucket you won't get the export data because Amazon S3 doesn't have permission to write to the destination bucket. If the source bucket is owned by a different account than that of the current user, then the correct account ID of the source bucket must be substituted in the policy.

```
{
    "Id": "S3-Console-Auto-Gen-Policy·          ",
    "Version": "2012-10-17",
    "Statement": [
        {
            "Sid": "S3PolicyStmt-DO-NOT-MODIFY-          7",
            "Effect": "Allow",
            "Principal": {
                "Service": "s3.amazonaws.com"
            },
            "Action": [
```

Amazon S3 could not create a bucket policy on the destination bucket. ✕

Ask the destination bucket owner to add the following bucket policy to allow Amazon S3 to place data in that bucket. Learn more

For information about the exported data and how the filter works, see Amazon S3 Analytics – Storage Class Analysis in the *Amazon Simple Storage Service Developer Guide*.

More Info
Storage Management

How Do I Configure Amazon S3 Inventory?

Amazon S3 inventory provides a flat file list of your objects and metadata, which is a scheduled alternative to the Amazon S3 synchronous `List` API operation. Amazon S3 inventory provides comma-separated values (CSV) or Apache optimized row columnar (ORC) output files that list your objects and their corresponding metadata on a daily or weekly basis for an S3 bucket or for objects that share a prefix (objects that have names that begin with the same string). For more information, see Amazon S3 Inventory in the *Amazon Simple Storage Service Developer Guide*.

To configure inventory

1. Sign in to the AWS Management Console and open the Amazon S3 console at https://console.aws.amazon.com/s3/.

2. In the **Bucket name** list, choose the name of the bucket for which you want to configure Amazon S3 inventory.

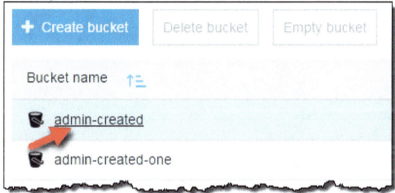

3. Choose the **Management** tab, and then choose **Inventory**.

4. Choose **Add new** if you do not have any inventory reports enabled.

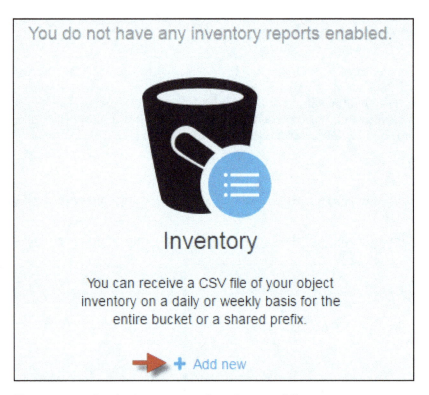

5. Type a name for the inventory and set it up as follows:

- Optionally, add a prefix for your filter to inventory only objects whose names begin with the same string.

- Choose the destination bucket where you want reports to be saved. The destination bucket must be in the same AWS Region as the bucket for which you are setting up the inventory. The destination bucket can be in a different AWS account.

- Optionally, choose a prefix for the destination bucket.

- Choose how frequently to generate the inventory.

6. Under **Advanced settings**, you can set the following:

1. Choose either the CSV or ORC output file format for your inventory. For more information about these formats, see Amazon S3 Inventory in the *Amazon Simple Storage Service Developer Guide*.

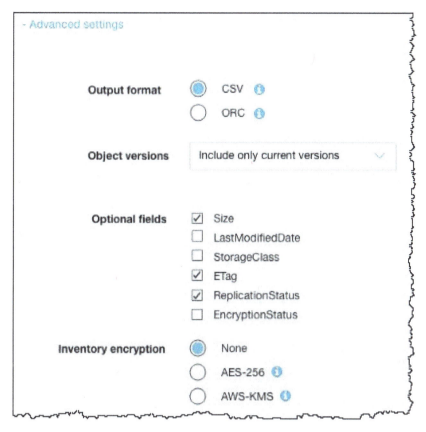

2. To include all versions of the objects in the inventory, choose **Include all versions** in the **Object versions** list. By default, the inventory includes only the current versions of the objects.

3. For **Optional fields**, select one or more of the following to add to the inventory report:

- **Size** – Object size in bytes.

- **Last modified date** – Object creation date or the last modified date, whichever is the latest.

- **Storage class** – Storage class used for storing the object.

- **ETag** – The entity tag is a hash of the object. The ETag reflects changes only to the contents of an object, and not its metadata. The ETag may or may not be an MD5 digest of the object data. Whether it is depends on how the object was created and how it is encrypted.

- **Replication status** – The cross-region replication status of the object. For more information, see How Do I Add a Cross-Region Replication (CRR) Rule to an S3 Bucket?

- **Encryption status** – The server-side encryption used to encrypt the object. For more information, see Protecting Data Using Server-Side Encryption in the *Amazon Simple Storage Service Developer Guide.*

For more information about the contents of an inventory report, see What's Included in an Amazon S3 Inventory? in the *Amazon Simple Storage Service Developer Guide.*

4. For **Encryption**, choose a server-side encryption option to encrypt the inventory report, or choose **None**:

- **None** – Do not encrypt the inventory report.

- **AES-256** – Encrypt the inventory report using server-side encryption with Amazon S3-managed keys (SSE-S3). Amazon S3 server-side encryption uses 256-bit Advanced Encryption Standard (AES-256). For more information, see Amazon S3-Managed Encryption Keys (SSE-S3) in the *Amazon Simple Storage Service Developer Guide.*

135

- **AWS-KMS** – Encrypt the report using server-side encryption with AWS KMS-managed keys (SSE-KMS). For more information, see AWS KMS–Managed Keys (SSE-KMS) in the *Amazon Simple Storage Service Developer Guide.* **Note**
  To encrypt the inventory list file with SSE-KMS, you must grant Amazon S3 permission to use the AWS KMS key. For instructions, see Grant Amazon S3 Permission to Encrypt Using Your AWS KMS Key.

7. Choose **Save**.

Destination Bucket Policy

Amazon S3 creates a bucket policy on the destination bucket that grants Amazon S3 write permission. This allows Amazon S3 to write data for the inventory reports to the bucket.

If an error occurs when you try to create the bucket policy, you are given instructions on how to fix it. For example, if you choose a destination bucket in another AWS account and don't have permissions to read and write to the bucket policy, you see the following message.

In this case, the destination bucket owner must add the displayed bucket policy to the destination bucket. If the policy is not added to the destination bucket, you won't get an inventory report because Amazon S3 doesn't have permission to write to the destination bucket. If the source bucket is owned by a different account than that of the current user, the correct account ID of the source bucket must be substituted in the policy.

For more information, see Amazon S3 Inventory in the *Amazon Simple Storage Service Developer Guide.*

Grant Amazon S3 Permission to Encrypt Using Your AWS KMS Key

You must grant Amazon S3 permission to encrypt using your AWS KMS key with a key policy. The following procedure describes how to use the AWS Identity and Access Management (IAM) console to modify the key policy for the AWS KMS customer master key (CMK) that is being used to encrypt the inventory file.

To grant permissions to encrypt using your AWS KMS key

1. Sign in to the AWS Management Console using the AWS account that owns the AWS KMS CMK. Open the IAM console at https://console.aws.amazon.com/iam/.

2. In the left navigation pane, choose **Encryption keys**.

3. For **Region**, choose the appropriate AWS Region. Do not use the region selector in the navigation bar (upper-right corner).

4. Choose the alias of the CMK that you want to encrypt inventory with.

5. In the **Key Policy** section of the page, choose **Switch to policy view**.

6. Using the **Key Policy** editor, insert following key policy into the existing policy and then choose **Save Changes**. You might want to copy the policy to the end of the existing policy.

```
1  {
2      "Sid": "Allow Amazon S3 use of the key",
3      "Effect": "Allow",
4      "Principal": {
5          "Service": "s3.amazonaws.com"
6      },
7      "Action": [
8          "kms:GenerateDataKey*"
9      ],
10     "Resource": "*"
11 }
```

For more information about creating and editing AWS KMS CMKs, see Getting Started in the *AWS Key Management Service Developer Guide*.

More Info
Storage Management

How Do I Configure Request Metrics for an S3 Bucket?

There are two types of CloudWatch metrics for Amazon S3: storage metrics and request metrics. Storage metrics are reported once per day and are provided to all customers at no additional cost. Request metrics are available at 1-minute intervals after some latency to process, and metrics are billed at the standard CloudWatch rate. To get request metrics, you must opt into them by configuring them in the console or with the Amazon S3 API.

For more conceptual information about CloudWatch metrics for Amazon S3, see Monitoring Metrics with Amazon CloudWatch in the *Amazon Simple Storage Service Developer Guide*.

To configure request metrics on a bucket

1. Sign in to the AWS Management Console and open the Amazon S3 console at https://console.aws.amazon.com/s3/.

2. In the **Bucket name** list, choose the name of the bucket that has the objects you want to get request metrics for.

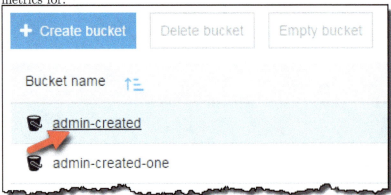

3. Choose the **Management** tab, and then choose **Metrics**.

4. Choose **Requests**.

5. From the name of your bucket in the left-side pane, choose the edit icon.

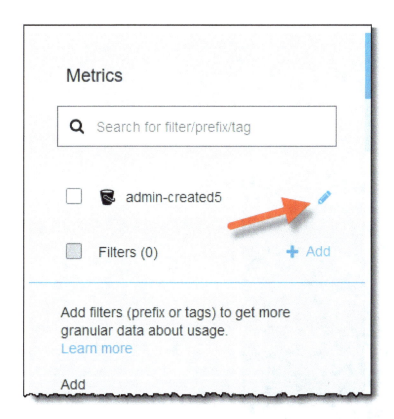

6. Choose the **Request metrics** check box. This also enables Data Transfer metrics.

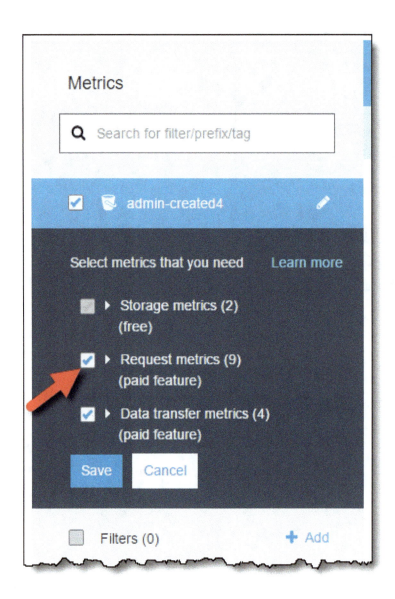

7. Choose **Save**.

You have now created a metrics configuration for all the objects in an Amazon S3 bucket. About 15 minutes after CloudWatch begins tracking these request metrics, you can see graphs for the metrics in both the Amazon S3 or CloudWatch consoles. You can also define a filter so the metrics are only collected and reported on a subset of objects in the bucket. For more information, see How Do I Configure a Request Metrics Filter?.

How Do I Configure a Request Metrics Filter?

There are two types of CloudWatch metrics for Amazon S3: storage metrics and request metrics. Storage metrics are reported once per day and are provided to all customers at no additional cost. Request metrics are available at 1 minute intervals after some latency to process, and metrics are billed at the standard CloudWatch rate. To get request metrics, you must opt into them by configuring them in the console or with the Amazon S3 API.

For more conceptual information about CloudWatch metrics for Amazon S3, see Monitoring Metrics with Amazon CloudWatch in the *Amazon Simple Storage Service Developer Guide.*

To filter request metrics on a subset of objects in a bucket

1. Sign in to the AWS Management Console and open the Amazon S3 console at https://console.aws.amazon.com/s3/.

2. In the **Bucket name** list, choose the name of the bucket that has the objects you want to get request metrics for.

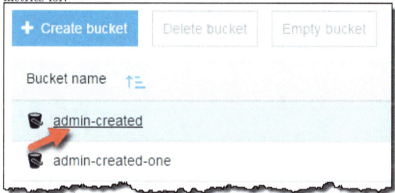

3. Choose the **Management** tab. and then choose **Metrics**.

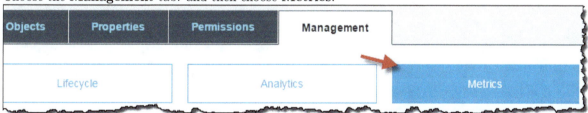

4. Choose **Requests**.

5. From **Filters** in the left-side pane, choose **Add**.

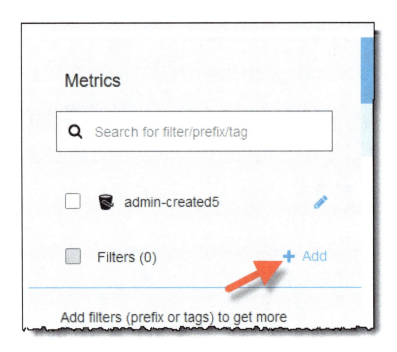

6. Provide a name for this metrics configuration.

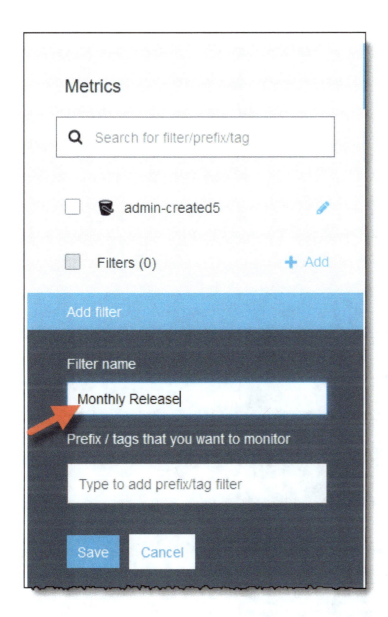

7. Provide one or more prefixes or tags, separated by commas, in **Prefix /tags that you want to monitor**. From the drop down, select whether the value you provided is a tag or a prefix.

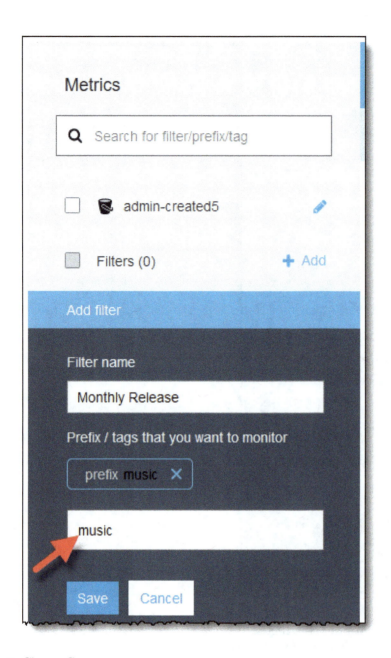

8. Choose **Save**.

You have now created a metrics configuration for request metrics on a subset of the objects in an Amazon S3 bucket. About 15 minutes after CloudWatch begins tracking these request metrics, you can see graphs for the metrics in both the Amazon S3 or CloudWatch consoles. You can also request metrics at the bucket level. For information, see How Do I Configure Request Metrics for an S3 Bucket?

Setting Bucket and Object Access Permissions

The topics in this section explain how to use the Amazon S3 console to grant access permissions to your buckets and objects by using resource-based access policies. An access policy describes who has access to resources. You can associate an access policy with a resource.

Buckets and objects are Amazon Simple Storage Service (Amazon S3) resources. By default, all Amazon S3 resources are private, which means that only the resource owner can access the resource. The resource owner is the AWS account that creates the resource. For more information about resource ownership and access policies, see Overview of Managing Access in the *Amazon Simple Storage Service Developer Guide.*

Bucket access permissions specify which users are allowed access to the objects in a bucket and which types of access they have. *Object access permissions* specify which users are allowed access to the object and which types of access they have. For example, one user might have only read permission, while another might have read and write permissions.

Bucket and object permissions are independent of each other. An object does not inherit the permissions from its bucket. For example, if you create a bucket and grant write access to a user, you will not be able to access that user's objects unless the user explicitly grants you access.

To grant access to your buckets and objects to other AWS accounts and to the general public, you use resource-based access policies called access control lists (ACLs).

A *bucket policy* is a resource-based AWS Identity and Access Management (IAM) policy that grants other AWS accounts or IAM users access to an S3 bucket. Bucket policies supplement, and in many cases, replace ACL-based access policies. For more information on using IAM with Amazon S3, see Managing Access Permissions to Your Amazon S3 Resources in the *Amazon Simple Storage Service Developer Guide.*

For more in-depth information about managing access permissions, see Introduction to Managing Access Permissions to Your Amazon S3 Resources in the *Amazon Simple Storage Service Developer Guide.*

This section also explains how to use the Amazon S3 console to add a cross-origin resource sharing (CORS) configuration to an S3 bucket. CORS allows client web applications that are loaded in one domain to interact with resources in another domain.

Identifying Public Buckets Using Bucket Permissions Check

Bucket permissions check in the Amazon S3 console checks bucket policies and bucket access control lists (ACLs) to identify publicly accessible buckets. *Publicly accessible* is defined as accessible by either everyone in the world or by any authenticated AWS user.

Access is defined as the ability to either read or write objects to the buckets, edit bucket permissions, or perform other Amazon S3 operations. *Reading* a bucket means listing the objects that are stored in the bucket, and *writing* means being able to upload/PUT objects into the bucket.

There are two ways that S3 buckets can be made publicly accessible: through bucket policies and ACLs. For more information about bucket policies, ACLs, and permissions, see Managing Access Permissions to Your Amazon S3 Resources in the *Amazon Simple Storage Service Developer Guide.*

Bucket permissions check does not check object ACLs, which can allow everyone in the world or any authenticated AWS user to access the object and its permissions. An object can also be publicly accessible through the object's ACLs. When an object is publicly accessible through the READ ACL, it allows access to the contents of the object. With READ_ACP and WRITE_ACP ACLs, grantees can also read and modify the object ACLs respectively.

Bucket permissions check makes it easier to identify S3 buckets that provide public read and write access. You can also view whether the source for the public access is a bucket policy, a bucket ACL, or both. If you change a bucket policy or a bucket ACL, the Amazon S3 console analyzes them in real time and alerts you if those changes enable public read and write access on the bucket.

Listing Public Buckets

The List buckets view now shows whether your bucket is publicly accessible. Amazon S3 labels the permissions for a bucket as follows:

- **Public** – Publicly accessible by either everyone in the world or by any authenticated AWS user.

- **Not public*** – The bucket is not publicly accessible. However, objects in the bucket might be publicly accessible due to object ACLs.

- **Access denied** – Locked out of the bucket.

- **Error** – A service-related error occurred.

- **Undetermined**– Amazon S3 cannot determine whether the bucket is publicly accessible.

To get a list of the public buckets with public read and write access, choose the orange **Public** button next to the number of buckets.

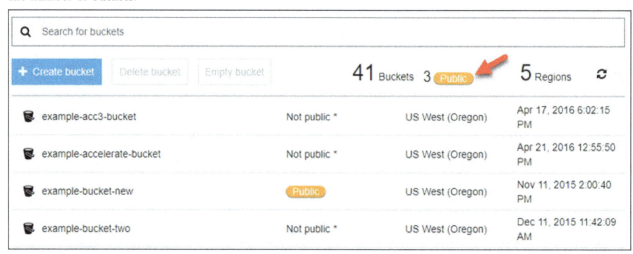

You can also get a list with more specific access information. In the **Search for buckets** bar drop-down list, choose **Buckets with any public access (read/write)**, **Buckets with public read access**, or **Buckets with public write access**.

If you choose either the orange **Public** button or **Buckets with any public access (read/write)**, you see a list of the public buckets with information about **Read** and **Write** access permissions.

To change this list to show only **Read** or only **Write** access permissions, choose the **X** on the **Public:Read** or **Public:Write** buttons that are located above the list. If you choose the** X** on both, you return to the List all buckets page.

The **Source** column shows whether the bucket is marked as public because of an **ACL** or a **Bucket policy**, or both. **ACL** and **Bucket policy** are links—choose the link to view the permissions page, which shows why the bucket is marked public. You can then change the permission if needed. For more information on changing ACL and bucket policy permission, see How Do I Set ACL Bucket Permissions? and How Do I Add an S3 Bucket Policy?.

More Info

- Setting Bucket and Object Access Permissions
- How Do I Set ACL Bucket Permissions?
- How Do I Add an S3 Bucket Policy?

How Do I Set Permissions on an Object?

This section explains how to use the Amazon Simple Storage Service (Amazon S3) console to manage access permissions for an S3 object by using access control lists (ACLs). ACLs are resource-based access policies that grant access permissions to buckets and objects. For more information about managing access permissions with resource-based policies, see Overview of Managing Access in the *Amazon Simple Storage Service Developer Guide.*

Bucket and object permissions are independent of each other. An object does not inherit the permissions from its bucket. For example, if you create a bucket and grant write access to a user, you can't access that user's objects unless the user explicitly grants you access.

You can grant permissions to other AWS accounts or predefined groups. The user or group that you grant permissions to is called the grantee. By default, the owner, which is the AWS account that created the bucket, has full permissions.

Each permission you grant for a user or a group adds an entry in the ACL that is associated with the object. The ACL lists grants, which identify the grantee and the permission granted. For more information about ACLs, see Managing Access with ACLs in the *Amazon Simple Storage Service Developer Guide.*

To set permissions for an object

1. Sign in to the AWS Management Console and open the Amazon S3 console at https://console.aws.amazon. com/s3/.

2. In the **Bucket name** list, choose the name of the bucket that contains the object.

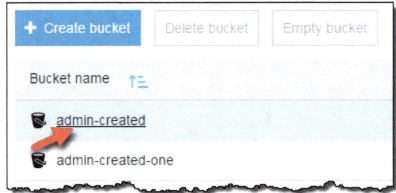

3. In the **Name** list, choose the name of the object for which you want to set permissions.

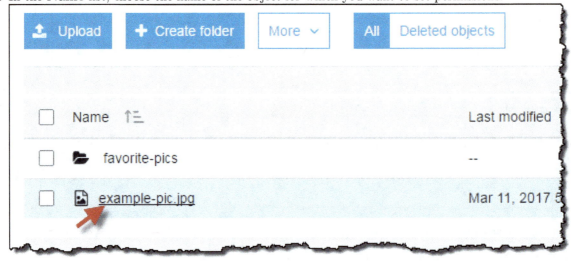

4. Choose **Permissions**.

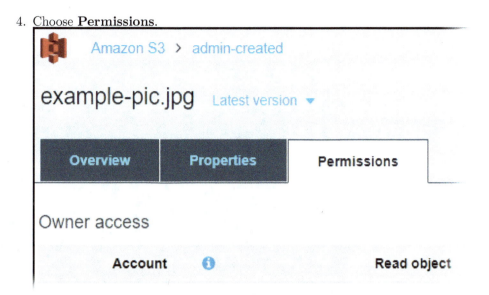

5. You can manage object access permissions for the following:

   1.

Owner access

1 The *owner* refers to the AWS account root user, and not an AWS Identity and Access Management
       \(IAM\) user\. For more information about the root user, see [The AWS Account Root User](
       http://docs.aws.amazon.com/IAM/latest/UserGuide/id_root-user.html)\.

2

3 To make changes to the owner's object access permissions, under **Owner access**, choose the
       account name, which is the name of the AWS account root user\.

4

5 Select the check boxes for the permissions that you want to change, and then choose **Save**\.

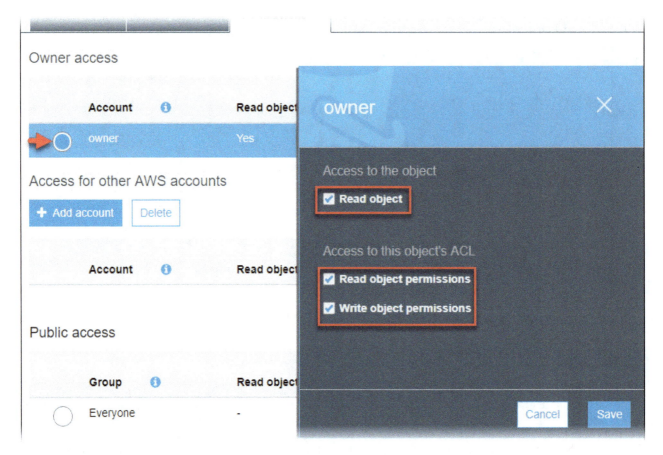

1.

Access for other AWS accounts

1 To grant permissions to an AWS user from a different AWS account, under **Access for other AWS accounts**, choose **Add account**\. In the **Enter an ID** field, type the canonical ID of the AWS user that you want to grant object permissions to\. For information about finding a canonical ID, see [AWS Account Identifiers](http://docs.aws.amazon.com/general/latest/gr/acct-identifiers.html) in the *Amazon Web Services General Reference*\. You can add as many as 99 users\.

2

3 Select the check boxes for the permissions that you want to grant to the user, and then choose **Save**\. To display information about the permissions, choose the Help icons\.

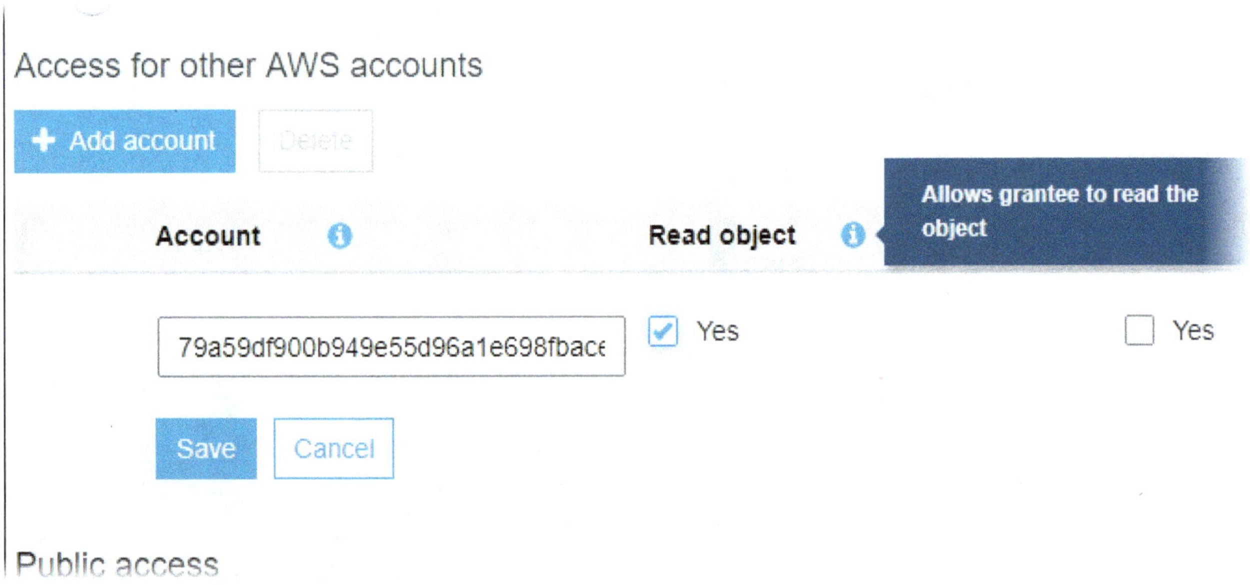

Access for other AWS accounts

+ Add account   Delete

Account ⓘ		Read object ⓘ	

> Allows grantee to read the object

79a59df900b949e55d96a1e698fbace   ☑ Yes   ☐ Yes

Save   Cancel

Public access

1.

Public access

1   To grant access to your object to the general public \(everyone in the world\), under **Public access**, choose **Everyone**\. Granting public access permissions means that anyone in the world can access the object\.

2

3   Select the check boxes for the permissions that you want to grant, and then choose **Save**\.

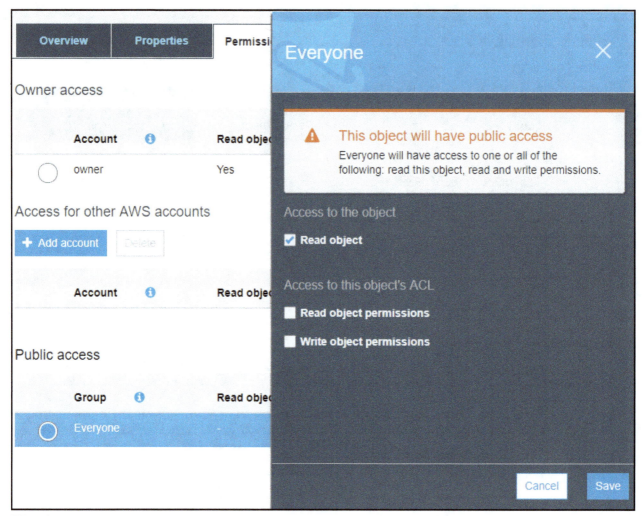

Warning

Use caution when granting the **Everyone** group anonymous access to your S3 objects. When you grant access to this group, anyone in the world can access your bucket. If you need to grant access to everyone, we highly recommend that you only grant permissions to **Read objects**.

We highly recommend that you *do not* grant the **Everyone** group write object permissions. Doing so allows anyone to overwrite the ACL permissions for the object.

You can also set object permissions when you upload objects. For more information about setting permissions when uploading objects, see How Do I Upload Files and Folders to an S3 Bucket?.

More Info

- Setting Bucket and Object Access Permissions
- How Do I Set ACL Bucket Permissions?

How Do I Set ACL Bucket Permissions?

This section explains how to use the Amazon Simple Storage Service (Amazon S3) console to manage access permissions for S3 buckets by using access control lists (ACLs). ACLs are resource-based access policies that grant access permissions to buckets and objects. For more information about managing access permissions with resource-based policies, see Overview of Managing Access in the *Amazon Simple Storage Service Developer Guide*.

You can grant permissions to other AWS account users or to predefined groups. The user or group that you are granting permissions to is called the grantee. By default, the owner, which is the AWS account that created the bucket, has full permissions.

Each permission you grant for a user or group adds an entry in the ACL associated with the bucket. The ACL lists grants, which identify the grantee and the permission granted. For more information about ACLs, see Managing Access with ACLs in the *Amazon Simple Storage Service Developer Guide*.

To set ACL access permissions for an S3 bucket

1. Sign in to the AWS Management Console and open the Amazon S3 console at https://console.aws.amazon.com/s3/.

2. In the **Bucket name** list, choose the name of the bucket that you want to set permissions for.

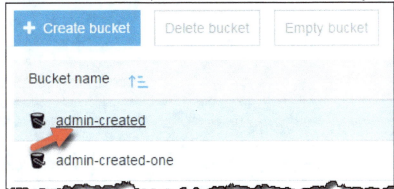

3. Choose **Permissions**.

4. You can manage bucket access permissions for the following:

   1.

Owner access

1 The *owner* refers to the AWS account root user, and not an AWS Identity and Access Management
     \(IAM\) user\. For more information about the root user, see [The AWS Account Root User](
     http://docs.aws.amazon.com/IAM/latest/UserGuide/id_root-user.html)\.

2

3 To make changes to the owner's bucket access permissions, under **Owner access**, choose the account name, which is the name of the AWS account root user\.

4

5 Select the check boxes for the permissions that you want to change, and then choose **Save**\.

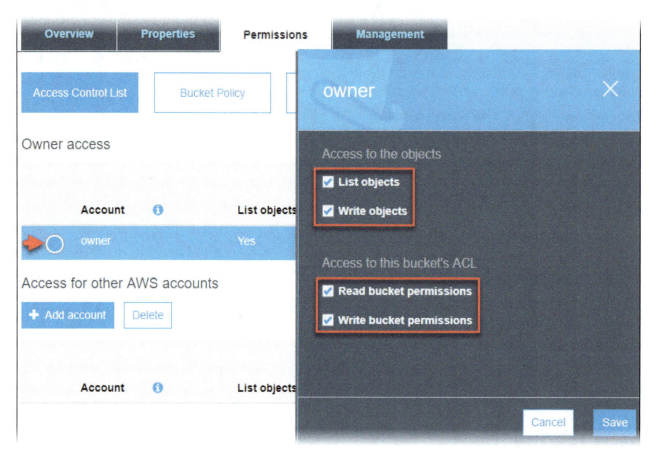

1.

Access for other AWS accounts

1 To grant permissions to an AWS user from a different AWS account, under **Access for other AWS accounts**, choose **Add account**\. In the **Enter an ID** field, type the canonical ID of the AWS user that you want to grant bucket permissions to\. For information about finding a canonical ID, see [AWS Account Identifiers](http://docs.aws.amazon.com/general/latest/gr/acct-identifiers.html) in the *Amazon Web Services General Reference*\. You can add as many as 99 users\.

2

3 Select the check boxes next to the permissions that you want to grant to the user, and then choose **Save**\. To display information about the permissions, choose the Help icons\.

154

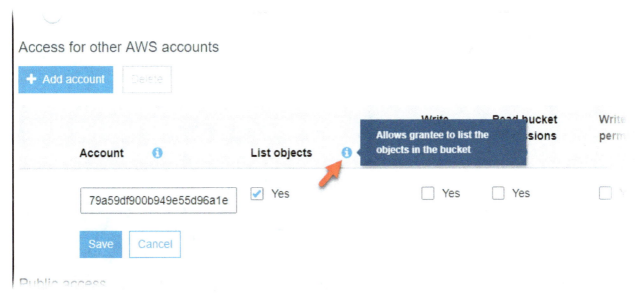

Warning

When you grant other AWS accounts access to your resources, be aware that the AWS accounts can delegate their permissions to users under their accounts. This is known as *cross-account access*. For information about using cross-account access, see Creating a Role to Delegate Permissions to an IAM User in the *IAM User Guide*.

1.

Public access

1. To grant access to your bucket to the general public \(everyone in the world\), under **Public access**, choose **Everyone**\. Granting public access permissions means that anyone in the world can access the bucket\.

2.

3. Select the check boxes for the permissions that you want to grant, and then choose **Save**\.

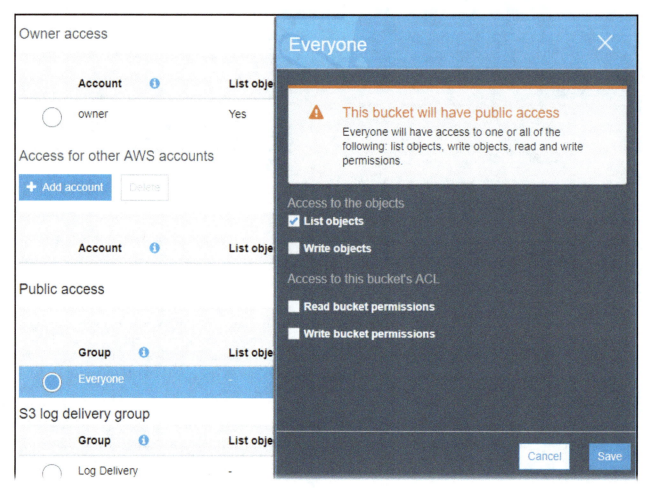

Warning

Use caution when granting the **Everyone** group public access to your S3 bucket. When you grant access to this group, anyone in the world can access your bucket. We highly recommend that you never grant any kind of public write access to your S3 bucket.

1.

S3 log delivery group

1   To grant access to Amazon S3 to write server access logs to the bucket, under **S3 log delivery group**, choose **Log Delivery**\.

2

3   If a bucket is set up as the target bucket to receive access logs, the bucket permissions must allow the **Log Delivery** group write access to the bucket\. When you enable server access logging on a bucket, the S3 console grants write access to the **Log Delivery** group for the target bucket that you choose to receive the logs\. For more information about server access logging, see [How Do I Enable Server Access Logging for an S3 Bucket ?](server-access-logging.md)\.

You can also set bucket permissions when you are creating a bucket. For more information on setting permissions when creating a bucket, see How Do I Create an S3 Bucket?.

More Info

- Setting Bucket and Object Access Permissions

- How Do I Set Permissions on an Object?
- How Do I Add an S3 Bucket Policy?

How Do I Add an S3 Bucket Policy?

This section explains how to use the Amazon Simple Storage Service (Amazon S3) console to add a new bucket policy or edit an existing bucket policy. A bucket policy is a resource-based AWS Identity and Access Management (IAM) policy. You add a bucket policy to a bucket to grant other AWS accounts or IAM users access permissions for the bucket and the objects in it. Object permissions apply only to the objects that the bucket owner creates. For more information about bucket policies, see Overview of Managing Access in the *Amazon Simple Storage Service Developer Guide*.

For examples of Amazon S3 bucket policies, see Bucket Policy Examples in the *Amazon Simple Storage Service Developer Guide*.

To create or edit a bucket policy

1. Sign in to the AWS Management Console and open the Amazon S3 console at https://console.aws.amazon.com/s3/.

2. In the **Bucket name** list, choose the name of the bucket that you want to create a bucket policy for or whose bucket policy you want to edit.

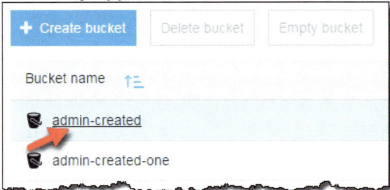

3. Choose **Permissions**, and then choose **Bucket Policy**.

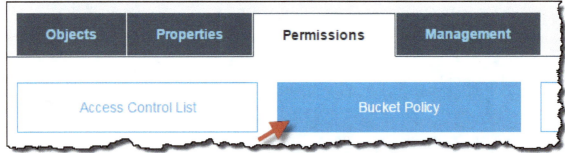

4. In the **Bucket policy editor** text box, type or copy and paste a new bucket policy, or edit an existing policy. The bucket policy is a JSON file. The text you type in the editor must be valid JSON.

5. Choose **Save**. **Note**

Amazon S3 displays the Amazon Resource Name (ARN) for the bucket next to the **Bucket policy editor** title. For more information about ARNs, see Amazon Resource Names (ARNs) and AWS Service Namespaces in the *Amazon Web Services General Reference*.

Directly below the bucket policy editor text box is a link to the **Policy Generator**, which you can use to create a bucket policy.

More Info

- Setting Bucket and Object Access Permissions
- How Do I Set ACL Bucket Permissions?

How Do I Allow Cross-Domain Resource Sharing with CORS?

This section explains how to use the Amazon S3 console to add a cross-origin resource sharing (CORS) configuration to an S3 bucket. CORS allows client web applications that are loaded in one domain to interact with resources in another domain.

To configure your bucket to allow cross-origin requests, you add CORS configuration to the bucket. A CORS configuration is an XML document that defines rules that identify the origins that you will allow to access your bucket, the operations (HTTP methods) supported for each origin, and other operation-specific information. For more information about CORS, see Cross-Origin Resource Sharing (CORS) in the *Amazon Simple Storage Service Developer Guide*.

When you enable CORS on the bucket, the access control lists (ACLs) and other access permission policies continue to apply.

To add a CORS configuration to an S3 bucket

1. Sign in to the AWS Management Console and open the Amazon S3 console at https://console.aws.amazon.com/s3/.

2. In the **Bucket name** list, choose the name of the bucket that you want to create a bucket policy for.

3. Choose **Permissions**, and then choose **CORS configuration**.

4. In the **CORS configuration editor** text box, type or copy and paste a new CORS configuration, or edit an existing configuration. The CORS configuration is an XML file. The text that you type in the editor must be valid XML.

5. Choose **Save**. **Note**
   Amazon S3 displays the Amazon Resource Name (ARN) for the bucket next to the **CORS configuration editor** title. For more information about ARNs, see Amazon Resource Names (ARNs) and AWS Service Namespaces in the *Amazon Web Services General Reference*.

More Info

- Setting Bucket and Object Access Permissions
- How Do I Set ACL Bucket Permissions?
- How Do I Add an S3 Bucket Policy?

Document History

The following table describes the important changes to the documentation since the last release of the *Amazon Simple Storage Service Console User Guide*.

Relevant Dates to this History:

- **Last documentation update:** November 17, 2017

Change	Description	Date Changed
Support for ORC-formatted Amazon S3 inventory files	Amazon S3 now supports the Apache optimized row columnar (ORC) format in addition to comma-separated values (CSV) file format for inventory output files. For more information, see How Do I Configure Amazon S3 Inventory?.	In this release
Bucket permissions check	Bucket permissions check in the Amazon S3 console checks bucket policies and bucket access control lists (ACLs) to identify publicly accessible buckets. Bucket permissions check makes it easier to identify S3 buckets that provide public read and write access. For more information, see Identifying Public Buckets Using Bucket Permissions Check.	November 06, 2017
Default encryption for S3 buckets	Amazon S3 default encryption provides a way to set the default encryption behavior for an S3 bucket. You can set default encryption on a bucket so that all objects are encrypted when they are stored in the bucket. The objects are encrypted using server-side encryption with either Amazon S3-managed keys (SSE-S3) or AWS KMS-managed keys (SSE-KMS). For more information, see How Do I Enable Default Encryption for an S3 Bucket?.	November 06, 2017

Change	Description	Date Changed
Encryption status in Amazon S3 inventory	Amazon S3 now supports including encryption status in Amazon S3 inventory so you can see how your objects are encrypted at rest for compliance auditing or other purposes. You can also configure to encrypt Amazon S3 inventory with server-side encryption (SSE) or SSE-KMS so that all inventory files are encrypted accordingly. For more information, see How Do I Configure Amazon S3 Inventory?.	November 06, 2017
Cross-region replication enhancements	Cross-region replication now supports the following: [See the AWS documentation website for more details]	November 06, 2017
Added functionality and documentation	The Amazon S3 console now supports enabling object-level logging for an S3 bucket with AWS CloudTrail data events logging. For more information, see How Do I Enable Object-Level Logging for an S3 Bucket with AWS CloudTrail Data Events?.	October 19, 2017
Old Amazon S3 console no longer available	The old version of the Amazon S3 console is no longer available and the old user guide was removed from the Amazon S3 documentation site.	August 31, 2017
General availability of New Amazon S3 console	Announced the general availability of the new Amazon S3 console.	May 15, 2017

AWS Glossary

For the latest AWS terminology, see the AWS Glossary in the *AWS General Reference*.

www.ingramcontent.com/pod-product-compliance
Lightning Source LLC
LaVergne TN
LVHW082039050326
832904LV00005B/236